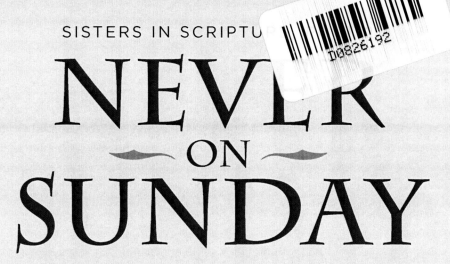

SISTERS IN SCRIPTU

NEVER
~ ON ~
SUNDAY

A Look at the Women NOT in the Lectionary

KATHLEEN MacINNIS KICHLINE

This book is lovingly dedicated in gratitude to that long line of women whose example of faithfulness to God has passed along courage, hope and love—especially those whose lives most immediately touched ours: mothers, grand and great-grand mothers, aunts, mentors, and teachers. It is further dedication to those who will follow—our own sisters, daughters, granddaughters, students and other loved ones. May we con-spire to bring about the fullness of God's purpose in our lives.

—KATHLEEN MacINNIS KICHLINE
MARCH 17, 2011

Published by Kathleen MacInnis Kichline
www.sistersinscripture.com

The text is set in Charlemagne, Gotham, and Goudy Old Style.

Designed by Nelson Agustín
Printed and bound in the United States of America

ISBN 978-0-615-72891-9

CONTENTS

September 2010

Dear Scripture Scholar,

Welcome to **Never On Sunday: A Look at the Women NOT in the Lectionary**. This study was created as the sequel to **Sisters in Scripture: Exploring the Relationships of Biblical Women**. It uses the same model—background, prayer, reflection and study, and, once again, participants are invited to enter into the lives of the women studied even as they discover meaning for their own lives. The outcome this time, however, was a bit surprising.

Like a true younger sibling, **Never On Sunday** seemed determined from the start to assert her own identity. Perhaps it was because she focused on women who have been excluded, but a certain "attitude" quickly developed. Where one woman's voice might have remained unheard, the combined, collective stories of these many women created the compelling question, "How could these women have been left out?" While we cannot answer that question, we can pull these amazing women out of obscurity. Their stories become our stories and speak with surprising clarity and relevancy to today's church. Maybe that explains her personality, but as you read, you will discover that **Never On Sunday** is decidedly a bit sassy and, definitely, a lot fun.

Enjoy!

KATHLEEN MacINNIS KICHLINE, M. Div

NEVER ON SUNDAY

A Look at the Women NOT in the Lectionary

For over 40 years the Faithful at Mass have enjoyed hearing the Word of God on Sundays from the new lectionary. This 3-year cycle lectionary was first introduced on Palm Sunday, 1970, a result of the changes mandated by the Second Vatican Council. Many more books and passages of the Bible were thus made available to Catholics. Homilies have been based on these readings to demonstrate the connection between scripture and daily Christian life. This single fact has done much to contribute to the biblical literacy of Catholics and to nurture an interest in the study of the Sacred Scriptures.

Most Catholics, if asked, would likely assume that while some scripture had, of necessity, to be left behind, the lectionary represented the heart or "cream" of the Bible— that we were, in fact, getting essentially what was most important. In choosing what to include in the lectionary and what to leave out, there were, of course, consequences. One of the casualties of the choices made is that some significant biblical passages about women were omitted, relegated to weekday readings, or designated as optional.

This scripture study invites us to look at these stories left on the cutting room floor, those "left behind." Collectively, they represent a significant portion of biblical women. Their life stories, circumstances, and witness of faith will never be read aloud on a Sunday or developed in the homily. By retrieving these pieces, we reclaim an important portion of our heritage as daughters of the living God and followers of Jesus Christ.

In this scripture study, *Never on Sunday*, we will be given background material each week, read the appropriate scripture passages, prayerfully reflect upon them and respond to the reflection questions. When we come together as a group, we will share our responses, questions, and insights with one another and then use the tools of biblical scholarship to help us learn more about these particular stories and about the Bible as a whole.

NEVER ON SUNDAY

A Look at the Women NOT in the Lectionary

CALENDAR

OLD TESTAMENT

Week One	Five Women Who Saved Moses	_____
Week Two	Deborah	_____
Week Three	Naomi and Ruth	_____
Week Four	Huldah	_____
Week Five	Esther	_____
Week Six	Judith	_____
BREAK & Optional Retreat (see "Resources" at end)		
RETREAT		_____

NEW TESTAMENT

Week Seven	Mary in Unexpected Places	_____
Week Eight	The Bent Woman in Luke	_____
Week Nine	The Women who Followed Jesus	_____
Week Ten	Mary Magdalene at the Tomb	_____
Week Eleven	Women in the Early Church, I	_____
Week Twelve	Women in the Early Church, II	_____
RETREAT		_____

FACILITATOR'S PAGES

The heart of this study is the reflection questions and the sharing on them that occurs in the small group. The role of the facilitator is important in assuring the comfort of the participants by following the guidelines for sharing. It is also important to model participation by seriously undertaking the midweek work on the text. All participants are encouraged to hold one another in prayer throughout the week but this is a special task of the facilitator.

THE ROLE OF HOSPITALITY

In advance of participants' arrival these supplies should be set out:

- Sign-in sheet with names, address, phone number and e-mail
- Name-tags
- Pens and paper
- 1 or 2 "spare" Bibles
- Coffee, tea, etc.
- Refreshments
- Sign-in sheet for who will provide refreshments in coming weeks

WELCOME

Greet each person warmly, offering refreshments and having them create a name-tag and fill in the sign-in sheet. Check off the names of those you knew were coming, add the names of those you did not and, later, note the ones who'd been expected but did not come.

Once everyone is comfortable, begin by having everyone go around to introduce themselves—their name, their church affiliation or some other personal fact, and then 1) what previous experience they've had with scripture and 2) what their hopes are of this study.

OPENING PRAYER

Thank everyone for sharing and explain that we pray better when we are not strangers to one another. Explain that prayer together, and on our own, is an important part of this scripture study.

Invite participants to get comfortable and center themselves. Some suggestions for prayer:

- Your own spontaneous prayer
- Reading a favorite scripture selection, e.g. Psalm 139
- Singing a song
- When using the *Our Father*, mention ahead of time if you are using the doxology.
- Inviting a participant with the gift for leading prayer to do so   (ask this ahead of time)
- Reading the following (or some other prayer you want to share):

Good and gracious God, we gather together in your name and thank you for the many paths that have brought us here today. We thank you for your gift of Sacred Scripture; may we grow in our appreciation of that gift in our time together. We ask the guidance of your Holy Spirit as we consider the meaning of your Word in our lives and we ask for the gifts of wisdom, patience and love as we share our stories with one another. This we ask in Jesus' name. Amen.

OVERVIEW OF STUDY

If time allows, go over the introductory pages as a group. If not, encourage people to read them on their own in the coming week. Go over the "How to Use This Study at Home" so that all participants are prepared for the next gathering. If you cannot go over the guidelines for sharing this week, be sure to do so before sharing begins at the next meeting. Also, read aloud the bold paragraph just before the sharing guideline. Draw special attention to the selection "What is a Midrash" and encourage participants to try their hand at it and let them know that time will be taken each week to share any that are created. As the weeks progress, they will feel more comfortable with giving it a try.

Specifically remind the folks of what is to be done in the coming week: reading the scripture selection, praying, responding to the reflection questions, working on the Challenge Question or Midrash, and coming prepared to share next week.

Get sign-ups for refreshments, starting next week. Be sure everyone has your phone number. Let them know it's not too late to bring a friend.

CLOSING PRAYER

Explain and practice a "Squeeze Prayer" to close. This is an excellent way to close all the sessions should you choose to.

Everyone stands and joins hands. The ABC's are:

A = be Audible

B = be Brief

C = be Christ-centered

Start the prayer yourself, e.g.: "Thank you, Jesus for our time together. I ask you to bless each woman in the week ahead and help her find time her busy schedule to spend some time with scripture."

Then, squeeze the hand of the woman next to you who, similarly, voices a short prayer of thanks, request, praise, or contrition and then passes the squeeze along. Anyone can choose, instead, to simply pass the squeeze along wordlessly as well. When the squeeze comes back to you, end with, "Glory be to the Father, and to the Son, and to the Holy Spirit, Amen."

EXCERPT FROM
SISTERS IN SCRIPTURE

What makes it a scripture study?

It must contain both:

1) A critical look at the text, i.e., using the means of modern research and biblical scholarship tools:

- Historical setting
- Context
- Literary form
- Authorship

In this, we use as a guiding principle what our Church teaches about the use of scripture:

Since God speaks in Sacred Scripture through men in human fashion, (6) the interpreter of Sacred Scripture, in order to see clearly what God wanted to communicate to us, should carefully investigate what meaning the sacred writers really intended, and what God wanted to manifest by means of their words.

To search out the intention of the sacred writers, attention should be given, among other things, to "literary forms." For truth is set forth and expressed differently in texts which are variously historical, prophetic, poetic, or other forms of discourse. The interpreter must investigate what meaning the sacred writer intended to express and actually expressed in particular circumstances by using contemporary literary forms in accordance with the situation of his own time and culture. (7) For the correct understanding of what the sacred writer wanted to assert, due attention must be paid to the customary and characteristic styles of feeling,

speaking and narrating which prevailed at the time of the sacred writer, and to the patterns men normally employed at that period in their everyday dealings with one another. (8) But, since Holy Scripture must be read and interpreted in the sacred spirit in which it was written, (9) no less serious attention must be given to the content and unity of the whole of scripture if the meaning of sacred texts is to be correctly worked out. — *Dei Verbum*

2) **A personal and communal application** of what scripture means here and now. While we certainly want to look at what a story meant at the time it was composed, it is often more important to our faith life to know what the story can mean here and now. Scripture stories are not just about characters or history; they are more about our own lives—what we are being called to do in our own lives and in the life of our community. Thus, we will incorporate reflection questions that invite participants to apply the sacred texts to their own lives and then we will share what we learn with one another. All of this will be "hemmed in" with prayer—as we study at home and when we gather as a group.

It is our goal to use both the tools of scriptural scholarship and the discipline of prayerful reflection to break open the text for its meaning—or meanings. For the scriptural text always holds many layers of possible interpretation. It is not our purpose in this study to look for "right answers" but, rather, to encounter God's word as living and relevant. As scripture scholar Megan McKenna says, "We must begin the readings and the reflections with respect and honor the text, love it, and develop a relationship with it and with others, especially those who disagree with our thoughts about its meanings."

What makes it a women's scripture study?

Women attend, therefore, women's experiences, questions, and concerns drive the search for meaning and application in scripture. There's a natural tendency and dynamic for women in gathering to support one another's life and faith journey. We value that 2nd aspect of bible study, application to life experience, and will continually look for ways our prayers, relationships and faith walk can be enriched by the scriptures we encounter.

The subject of our study will not be limited to scriptures about women since all scripture is instructive and life-giving. We will, however, look at scripture for those stories, images, and meanings that are related to women's experiences and that might otherwise be overlooked or underdeveloped.

In this first round of scripture studies we will focus on the relationships between some women whose stories intersect in the Bible. Therefore, we will examine our own relationships as women.

What makes it a Catholic women's scripture study?

As Catholics, we approach the scriptures with that experience, awareness and intention. We are informed by our life experiences, our prayer life and our shared liturgical year and worship. As a parish faith community we have in common certain incidentals (e.g. having heard a particular song at Mass on Sunday) and, also, a foundational desire to share in realizing the presence of God in our midst as a parish.

Having said that, on one level, there is no such thing as a Catholic bible study. All the work that's been done in scripture studies since the mid 1900's has been ecumenical in nature. When Pope Pius XII opened up the field and encouraged Catholic scholars

in the 1940's, we joined mainline Protestants and Jews in a shared, respectful, exciting venture. For relative newcomers to the field, Catholics quickly made significant contributions through the work of scholars like Raymond E. Brown. Catholic scripture scholars do not represent a school of study as such but, rather, are contributors to the larger field. We will draw upon the work of scripture scholars from throughout the field of studies.

It is worth noting that, as Catholics, we do not believe that scripture should be interpreted literally.vAs such, we are at variance with more fundamentalist Protestant churches (and in alignment with most mainline Protestant churches). Given that the fundamentalist approach to the bible is prevalent in today's Christian culture and represents a large section of bible studies, there can be confusion around our Catholic, ecumenical approach. We are inspired by our fundamentalist brothers and sisters in their love of and enthusiasm for scripture and hope to grow in that regard in Catholics. We hope to be free of judgment around others' appropriation of God's word and seek for commonalities whenever possibility. We also seek to be free from literalism and rigidity of interpretation of our own sacred texts of Catholicism.

When we look for and discuss the relevance and meaning of a text, we will draw upon our shared Catholic experience, culture and imagination. As we believe in the importance of the role of tradition, we will look to it for insight and enrichment drawing upon our history, saints, writings and prayers as a resource for understanding.

NEVER ON SUNDAY: A LOOK AT THE WOMEN NOT IN THE LECTIONARY

How to Use this Study

At Home

The following four "movements" are suggested for your reading and reflecting on the scriptures. They can be done in four different time frames, in two or three, or all at once. In each case a prayerful attitude is important, aware that you are entering into the word of God and asking the Holy Spirit to guide and enlighten you.

1. Pray
   Read assigned scripture
   Make notes on questions that come to mind

2. Pray
   Read Background material
   Re-read assigned scripture

3. Pray
   Respond in written form to reflection questions

4. Pray
   Optional – Respond to CHALLENGE question or write a poem, midrash (see explanation, separate sheet) or create a picture in a medium of your choosing

In Group

- Gather, welcome, check-in, get refreshments and settle into small groups

- For Opening Prayer read prayer of that week together
- Group discussion on week's reading / reflection questions / share "challenge," Midrash
- End small group discussion at agreed upon time by sharing a Squeeze Prayer
- At break, get refreshments, etc. and then return to large group format
- "Closer Look at the Text" in large group
- Closing Prayer and FYI's for next week

You are invited to share in your small group, but you are not obligated to share your personal experiences. Whatever you chose to share is strictly voluntary. No one should share anything that causes discomfort or embarrassment to themselves or others. PLEASE answer each reflection question in the home study whether you share the response or not. This will enrich your own life and help you get all that you can out of the scripture study.

NEVER ON SUNDAY

TEN GUIDELINES FOR SHARING

1. Respect confidentiality. Repeat only your experience of a session—never another person's story, experiences or feelings.

2. Take time; allow every woman the chance to speak.

   - If you are an introvert, challenge yourself to speak up at least once or twice at every gathering.

   - If you are an extrovert, do not share more than two or three times until everyone has had the chance to speak.

3. Speak only for yourself drawing on your own experiences, feelings, insights and questions.

4. Use "I" statements, i.e. use phrases that are specific to you and not universal— e.g. avoid, "People always feel angry when that happens." Say, instead, "It makes me feel angry when that happens to me."

5. Suspend your sense of certainty.

6. Ask for what you need.

7. Give other people the space/time they need to experience their feelings.

8. Avoid "should." Do not give advice or problem solve.

9. "Thank you" is an appropriate response.

10. Silence is okay.

WHAT IS A MIDRASH?

In the Jewish tradition, a Midrash is a story about a story in the Bible. The belief is that there are a thousand different meanings to every biblical story. One saying goes that the Torah was not written with black ink on white parchment but with black flames upon white flames; that there is just as much truth in the spaces between the flames as there is in the flames. A Midrash fills in those holes or gaps like embroidery upon cloth. Often a Midrash seeks to answer some question that the story raises—for example, why did Lot's wife turn around? The people who tell such stories are *darshanim*, often rabbis or teachers, and the stories they tell are called Midrash. A Midrash recognizes that the best way to understand a story can be to make up a new story about it.

Each session of *Never on Sunday* invites you to create a Midrash. This may be an actual story about the story but can be any way of imaginatively entering the text and creating some way of expressing the truth, the wonder or the questions that it contains. One of the most common ways is to take on the voice of one of the characters and go from there. It can even be as simple as taking the form of a letter or dialogue. *There are sample midrashes in the Resources at the end of this book.*

Mediums other than words can also be used. You may be more comfortable with paints, clay, fabric, or music. Whatever your form of expression— maybe even one you've never tried before, would be an appropriate way to represent your encounter with the text. We are, after all, dealing with the Word of God, living and moving in our lives, and the Holy Spirit, the Source of all creativity. Who knows what we will be inspired to create?

NOTE: Another creative element of *Never on Sunday* is the boxed "Challenge" question at the end of the reflection questions. This is not necessarily meant to be shared, unless you choose to do so. It is meant for you to personally consider and try to answer in your own prayer life or journaling.

MIRIAM

AND

SHIPRAH, PUAH, JOCHEBED
AND **PHARAOH'S DAUGHTER:**

The Five Women Who Saved Moses

BACKGROUND:
MIRIAM

The Book of Exodus opens with the determination of the Pharaoh to rid Egypt of the children of Joseph who have become so numerous as to be seen as a threat. He focuses his attention on the male children and, in overlooking the females, he leaves his plan susceptible to the interventions of five women: the midwives, Shiphrah and Puah, Moses' mother, Jochebed, Pharaoh's own daughter, and Miriam, Moses' sister. All five end up coming together to assure the survival of the infant boy, Moses, who will become God's instrument for saving his people.

SHIPHRAH AND PUAH

How remarkable that the names of the two midwives have been preserved for us through several thousand years when we cannot ascertain with certainty the name of the Pharaoh who gave them the order to destroy Hebrew male babies. We cannot know for sure if Puah and Shiphrah were Hebrew or Egyptian. The names are Egyptian: *Puah*, meaning "childbearing or joy of parents" and *Shiphrah*, meaning "prolific or to procreate / or beauty." Even their names attest to their role of ushering in life. As midwives these women had learned to respect life and to honor the unseen forces at work in bringing to birth. They entered into the private lives and homes of the women they assisted and, no doubt, spoke of very personal things. If not Hebrews themselves, they'd likely heard the mothers call out in prayer to their God, Yahweh, in the birth process. They had learned to respect both life and this Hebrew God. In addition to being midwives, themselves, they were, most likely, the overseers of the many midwives needed to assist at birth.

This would explain Pharaoh's call upon them. He commands them to put to death all the male children born to the Hebrews. This is genocide prompted, scholars suggest, by the hostile border pressure of Semitic tribes, the same stock as the Hebrews. Shiphrah and

Puah, slaves or those who attend to slaves, are called into the presence of the Pharaoh and personally charged to be sure this happens. This creates an impossible dilemma: obey the supreme ruler at the risk of their lives or violate all that they believe.

Their solution is both creative and somewhat humorous. No doubt they arrived at it as a result of prayer. Realizing that the presence of the midwives was more dangerous to the newborn than was their absence, they procrastinated their arrival until well after the baby's sex was declared and it was then too late to clandestinely dispose of the child. Later when Pharaoh calls them on the carpet, they play upon his male ignorance and, perhaps, racial prejudice, in claiming that the birth process is different for the "robust" Hebrews who give birth before they arrive. The Pharaoh buys their story but then escalates the command to include not only midwives but all his subjects who are to "throw into the river every boy born to the Hebrews." (1:22)

JOCHEBED AND PHARAOH'S DAUGHTER

We know the name of Moses' mother from Ex 6:20 and Num 26:59—*Jochebed*, a name meaning, "Yahweh is glory." It is hard to imagine the desperation of a mother in Jochebed's situation. Reminded, perhaps, of how Yahweh spared Isaac, and maybe even aware of the habits of the royal household to bathe in the Nile, she hatches a plan. She consigns her infant son to the "river" but not as the Pharaoh commanded. She constructs a sturdy papyrus boat and lines it with pitch so that it is watertight and rides well upon the water. She then places him among the reeds where he will not drift away and instructs his older sister to watch over the baby. In the end her plan succeeds and she is able to serve as wetnurse to her own son for the three to four years that was typical in that time.

PHARAOH'S DAUGHTER

The name of Pharaoh's daughter is unknown. Some scholars speculate that she could have been the feminist Queen Hatshepsutm the half-sister to Thutmose III, who ruled Egypt in her own right. Others offer that she was one of Rameses II's fifty-nine daughters. At any rate she enjoys the privilege of disregarding her own father's edict and has a compassionate heart that "was moved with pity" (2:6). At first sight, she is aware that the child is Hebrew but this does not dissuade her. The immediate appearance of Miriam and the coincidence of a nearby nursing mother either do not arouse her suspicions or she is judicious enough to overlook them. At any rate, she adopts, names and raises Moses in the household of the Pharaoh from the time he is weaned at three or four. Not only is his life spared, but his exceptional upbringing later prepares him in a unique way for the leadership role he will take on.

MIRIAM

There are three episodes that feature Miriam. The first is the above scene where, nameless, she intercedes for her brother and saves his life.

The second episode is after the triumphant passage through the Red Sea, Ex 15:19-21, when she is introduced as Miriam, the sister of Aaron, and thereby the sister of Moses, and is also designated as "the prophetess Miriam." She takes on the role of leading the Hebrew women in a joyful dance of celebration.

The third episode occurs well into the desert experience when there is discord between Miriam and Aaron with their brother, Moses, Numbers 12:1-15. This story is complex and fraught with many questions. Make use of whatever footnotes are in your bible and come prepared to share the various explanations they offer.

Lastly, the death of Miriam is recorded in Num 20:1. Like her brothers, Moses (Dt 34:5) and Aaron (Num 20:29), she does not live to see the Promised Land. The three of them have served their purpose. Later, the prophet Micah will remind Israel, "I brought you up from Egypt, I set you free from the land of slavery, I sent Moses, Aaron, and Miriam to lead you." (Micah 6:4)

MIRIAM'S PRAYER

The prophetess Miriam, Aaron's sister, took a tambourine in her hand, while all the women went out after her with tambourines, dancing; and she led them in the refrain: Sing to the Lord, for he is gloriously triumphant; horse and chariot he has thrown into the sea. Ex 15:20-21

Miriam leads the people in a joyous dance of praise to Yahweh for the delivery they have just experienced. Theirs is an outpouring of exuberant release and relief. By finding words to convey the emotion and inviting others to join in, Miriam provides her people with a way to memorialize the event and to praise God.

Dance with us, O God of Miriam,

Fill us with awareness and wonder for all You have done for us.

Give us grateful hearts and a joyful spirit

that comes from acknowledging your goodness.

We are free, we are free

because you have stretched out Your hand to save us.

May we never forget that You have loved us.

May we never forget that You are mighty

May we always know that You are near.

Let us sing of your goodness and tell of your deeds.

Let us join with others in proclaiming your name.

Our voices together delight your ears.

Our hands clasped together are held in your own.

We are your people and You are our God.

Amen.

- KMcK

NEVER ON SUNDAY
A Look at the Women NOT in the Lectionary

WEEK ONE - MIRIAM

Ex 1:5-2:10

PUAH AND SHIPHRAH

Recall your own experiences around childbirth—yours or the care of another. How did that affect your view of life? Can you think of someone who disobeyed authority but did what was right? Have you ever been in a situation that conflicted with your values? How did it feel? What did you do? Who do you see as modern day Puahs and Shiphrahs?

JOCHEBED

What do you think inspired Moses' mother to come up with the papyrus boat "solution?" Do you think there are women today in such desperate situations for their children—willing to "lose" them so they can live? How do you think Jochebed used the 3-4 years she had with Moses to prepare him for his later life?

PHARAOH'S DAUGHTER

Do you think Pharoah's daughter suspected Miriam or her mother's identity or not? Why? Does this story remind you of any other adoption stories? Can you think of an example of someone who has used their authority and influence to intercede for others?

MIRIAM

1) Miriam was about seven years old when she interceded for her infant brother with the pharaoh's daughter. Can you recall early signs in your life of your own potential for leadership or courage? How or how not was that received and developed? What other early characteristics shaped your values and identity?

Ex 15:1-21

2) *Recall any "Exodus" events in your own life, times when God has freed you from what had oppressed you. How did you celebrate? What was your refrain? Who are the others with whom you "dance?"*

Num 12:1-15

3) *What do you think were the real motives of Miriam and Aaron in speaking against Moses?*

4) *Do you feel God dealt justly with Miriam and Aaron?*

5) *What does Moses' reaction tell you about him, about his relationship with his sister?*

6) *Some commentators say that Aaron was not afflicted with leprosy because he was a priest; others say this shows how women who transgress are always treated more harshly then men.*

What do you think?

What do your think Miriam's thoughts were in her confinement? How do you picture the response of the people?

7) *How well do you come to know Miriam by the end of the story?*

8) *The women play a pivotal role in the story of Moses and, subsequently, the Exodus. How do you see women work together to protect life, and those most vulnerable?*

Some ideas for a Midrash: How did Miriam and Moses reunite and what was it like? Imagine the conversation between Jochebed, her husband and Miriam when she decides to hide Moses. Imagine a scene or situation that shows Miriam as a prophetess. What did the Hebrew women say to one another about Miriam's leprosy?

CHALLENGE

Think of a mother you may know of who has young children and is in need. Pray about how to respond to her situation and resolve to do something nice for her—maybe a gift basket, a casserole meal or an offer to babysit. Pray for her and her children.

A CLOSER LOOK AT THE TEXT:
MIRIAM

THE EXODUS EVENT, ITS CONTEXT AND IMPORTANCE

The first five books of the Bible are referred to as the Pentateuch or, to Jews, the Torah, and they are Genesis, Exodus, Leviticus, Numbers and Deuteronomy. Together they comprise the heart of the Hebrew Scriptures because they tell the story of the covenant. Set within the universal context starting at creation, the Pentateuch tells the story of God's selecting a certain people and entering into relationship, a covenant, with them and all that that ends up entailing. As they agree to take on the responsibilities to worship and obey only this God, they are formed by that into a distinct nation, united by faith more than by blood.

The present structure of these five books has a definite shape. At the center stands the giving of the law on Mount Sinai in all its detail:

Genesis 1-11 – *Human Origins*
Divine blessing, sin, punishment and mercy

Genesis 12-50 – *The Patriarchs*
Divine election, promise of progeny, land and greatness

Exodus 1-18 – *God Saves His People*
The Exodus, God saves Israel and begins the fulfillment of the promise of land.

Exodus 19-24, The Book of Leviticus, Numbers 1-10 –
God's People Receive the Law
The Covenant embodied in the Law binds Yahweh and Israel together forever and establishes a way of life.

Numbers 11-36 – *Journey to the Promised Land*
God leads the people to the promised land but punishes rebellion.

The Book of Deuteronomy – *Final Words of Moses*
Moses' final warnings to obey the covenant or lose the land.

The rest of the Old Testament can be divided into three categories: the Historical Books, The Wisdom Books and the Prophetical Books. They are grouped accordingly and come in that order. You may want to take a look at the listing of the books in the Table of Contents in your own bible to see how closely it corresponds to this breakdown.

The Hebrew Scriptures masterfully move through major themes presenting God's message. The first eleven chapters of Genesis address the great mysteries of the universe: how the world came to be, who God is, why God made us, the nature of good and evil, why there are a variety of peoples, etc. The rest of Genesis is given over to the remarkable story of how God chose to enter into relationship with a specific human being, Abraham, and, through Abraham, establish a covenant that would endure throughout time and complete God's plan for all creation. The great plan started out as a tiny flame in the promise to one person. Genesis faithfully chronicles the remarkable story of how that person and his family nurtured the flame and kept it alive through several generations. The focus, therefore, is on the family of Abraham, the patriarchs, and on the centrality of the Covenant.

With the Book of Exodus, the story moves on to how that Covenant is lived out, not in God's relationship with a particular family, but with how the Covenant is to be lived out in God's relationship with a whole people. The Book of Exodus and the Exodus event itself, is not only the major theme in scripture, it is foundational for the formation and identity of the people of God, who would later become the Jews.

It is with Moses that the transition is made. The God of Abraham, Isaac, and Jacob calls Moses to lead a whole people from slavery, into the dessert where the Covenant takes specific form, and to the Promised Land where the Covenant will be lived. With God's call to Moses comes an entirely new development. God intends to live out the promise to Abraham specifically with an entire nation.

Before this central event can take place, it takes the combined efforts of five women to ensure Moses' safe arrival in a troubled world. One of them, unnamed at the start, is his own sister. Her story will be linked with her brother, not only for her brave intervention as a child but also for her role as a partner with him in the Exodus event central to Judeo-Christianity.

MIRIAM'S ROLE IN ISRAEL'S HISTOR Y AND MEMORY

Miriam is not named until Ex 15: 20, "Miriam the prophetess, the sister of Aaron." This simple line tells the reader two things. In identifying her as the sister of Aaron, she is also the sister of Moses and her name is Miriam. The link is then made between Miriam of the desert and the young girl who boldly addressed the Pharaoh's daughter at the Nile. It also refers to her as a prophet, a term applied here before it is applied to Moses.

Miriam's title as a prophet and the role she takes on as the leader of the dance in the victory celebration may indicate that some forms of female authority, as in leading ritual, were in place in ancient Israelites but did not survive to later days. Women prophets continued to exist throughout the period of the Judges to follow, however (e.g. Huldah, 2 Kgs22:14, and Noadiah, Neh. 6:14).

When we read through episode of the Song of the Sea (Ex 15:1-21), it appears, at first glance to repeat itself. A close read of the scriptures often focuses on the dissonances which exist in the text. In other words, we need to pay special attention to those places where there's a bit of a speed bump as we read. Questions arise, like, "didn't they just say that already?" In verses1-18, we have the victory song sung after miraculously crossing through the Red Sea.

After Moses leads the Israelites in singing the song, there is a small fragment where the story is retold with Miriam leading the women in dance with her tambourine. Some scholars believe this seemingly extraneous piece of text represents the survival of an earlier version of the Exodus story wherein the Song of the Sea was probably sung by Miriam. This theory gained credence with the discovery of the Dead Sea Scrolls. One of the fragments found, 4Q365, when placed alongside the Song of the Sea, gives evidence of a longer Song of Miriam than the one existing in the two lines found in scripture today. The additional lines to the victory song include the phrase, "He exalted her to the heights"—an indication of Miriam's role in God's saving actions.

The song itself, and the story around it, was sung and re-sung for generations before being put into writing. The scriptures, as we have them, do not represent a seamless, chronological, as-it-happened narrative. They represent, rather, a painstaking piecing together of such stories, the first written form of which will not appear for about 400 years. The story of how the Hebrew, and, later, the Christian Scriptures, were put together is a topic we will return to in this study.

In Numbers 12:1-15 we have the peculiar and troubling story of Miriam and Aaron challenging Moses' authority and of Miriam's punishment with leprosy. At first their question seems logical, "Is it through Moses alone that God speaks? Does he not speak through us also?" (vs. 2). Moses had clearly shared his leadership with both of them, to some degree, and he had earlier said of others, besides himself, prophesying, "Would that all the people of God were prophets?" (Num. 11:29). There are, however—as is often the case, underlying issues, "Miriam and Aaron spoke against Moses on the pretext of the marriage he had contracted with a Cushite woman" (vs. 1). Whatever the cause, their complaint had to do with additional issues besides prophecy. God takes them in hand like an exasperated father saying, "Come out, you three, to the meeting tent" (vs. 3). The very fact that God dealt with them as siblings with some parity, underscores the complaint that Miriam and Aaron were making. Very quickly, however, God takes them to task and emphasizes the unique and superior role that Moses has to play.

Then Miriam is struck, in God's anger, with leprosy—a surprising and disconcerting turn of events! Aaron intercedes for her to Moses who turns to God in prayer for his sister. Again, there is anger in God's response but a proviso. The directive is given to confine her for seven days and, after that she may be restored.

Both Miriam and Aaron are, indeed, guilty as charged. Why, then, is Miriam stricken but not Aaron? Answers frequently center around issues of gender. The answer can either be seen as 1) reinforcement that women, in particular, should not overstep their authority or as 2) an example of how biased the text is in its treatment of women. Both of these viewpoints, while oppositional, deserve argument and consideration.

In addition to Miriam receiving punishment, we can focus on the exception of Aaron. He is the high priest and to strike him with leprosy would render him unclean and unable to perform priestly duties (Lev 22:4). As a non-priestly person, Miriam is expendable in a way that Aaron is not.

As close readers of the text, it might be helpful to employ the tool of "source criticism." Source criticism is one of the techniques of biblical scholars that looks at how a certain section was put together when, at last, an oral tradition was written down. In choosing to preserve this story and frame it in this particular way, the role of the priest, as well as the importance of Moses, is emphasized for a much-later Israel. As the paradigmatic priestly figure, the one from whom all priestly lineage was descended, Aaron could not be stricken with such a disease.

Additionally, Miriam's punishment may be seen, centuries later, as a "corrective" to any cultic role hinted at in the ancient text.

At any rate, Miriam enters into the seven-day confinement, justly or not. Such questions of fairness are not of interest to the biblical author. Her period of separation, however, allows her to address whatever her earlier issues were—jealousy, envy, pride... When she returns to her people her inner self is hopefully as cleansed as is her skin. "Miriam was confined outside the camp for seven days, and the people did not start out again until she was brought back." This may indicate not only that they did not proceed without her but that they would not proceed without her. Despite her position of leadership, she was not immune from the human frailties. Miriam was not perfect; nor were her brothers. Moses murdered an Egyptian and hid the fact (Ex 2:12) and Aaron fashioned a golden calf to worship (Ex 32:1-8).

Later in the Book of Numbers her death is recorded. "The whole Israelite community arrived in the desert of Zin in the first month, and the people settled at Kadesh. It was here that Miriam died, and here that she was buried." (Nm 20:1) There are, of course, strong water associations with Miriam: her vigil along the Nile watching over her infant brother and her victory dance after passing through the Red Sea. So, we need to take a close look at the line that follows the record of her death, "Now there was no water for the community..." The current numbering and spacing of scripture has a new paragraph begin with that phrase but no such break, or breaks of any kind, occurs in the original Hebrew. This inserted space creates a disassociation of Miriam's death with the drought that follows where it might be argued that the two are intentionally linked. The drought can be seen as the community mourning the loss of their leader, Miriam.

The memory of Miriam's presence and influence seems to have remained in the Israelite community as evidenced by references that have survived the years. Micah later reminds Israel of God's deliverance, "For I brought you up from the land of Egypt, from the place of slavery I released you; and I sent before you Moses, Aaron, and Miriam" (Micah 6:4). Her unfading memory is further attested to by the popularity of her name down through the years. "Mary' is the Hellenized version of the Hebraic "Miriam" and there are countless, significant women who have born that name down the years of our Judeo-Christian tradition.

Miriam starts out as the child mediator between an enslaved people and the household of a death-dealing Pharaoh. She emerges in the desert as a ritual leader and a prophet. She confronts Moses on issues of leadership and she loses. She is punished by God for the challenge and is silenced. But her name and her story are remembered and celebrated by the people throughout the ages.

MEANWHILE, ON SUNDAY MORNING....

The story of the two valiant midwives, **Shiphrah** and **Puah**, is entirely omitted from the lectionary. In the weekday readings, Monday of the Fifteenth Week in Ordinary Time, Year I, (lectionary #389), Exodus 1:8-22 is read but the selection skips from verse 14 to verse 22 leaving out the saving actions of these two brave women.

The story of the passage through the Red Sea is a part of the Easter Vigil reading (#42) but Ex 15:20-21 in which **Miriam** is identified as a prophet and leads the rejoicing at the sea is not included in the selected reading. The story of Miriam's jealousy and punishment with leprosy (Num. 12:1-13) is, however, recounted in a weekday reading, Tuesday of the 18th Week of Ordinary Time, Year I, (#408).

OLD TESTAMENT TIMELINE

AGE OF THE PATRIARCHS	1900	**BCE** **Abraham – Sarah & Hagar** **Isaac - Rebecca** **Jacob – Rachel & Leah** **Joseph**
EXODUS EXPERIENCE	1300 c.	**Moses / Exodus / Sinai Covenant**
PERIOD OF JUDGES	1250	**Invasion and settling of Canaan**

MONARCHY
    J – YAHWIST
 	
    E - ELOHIST
	1020
	
	922
		Saul, David, Solomon
		Divided Kingdom: Northern – Israel
		        Southern – Judah
		Prophets Amos (N), Hosea (N), Isaiah I (S), Micah (S)

	721	**Assyria conquers N. Kingdom - Israel**
D – DEUTERONOMIST		**Prophets** Jeremiah, Zephaniah, Nahum, Habakuk

EXILE
    P - PRIESTLY
	587	**Babylon conquers Judah**
		    Jerusalem destroyed
		    Leaders deported to Babylon
		Prophets Ezekiel, Isaiah II, Baruch

POST-EXILE JEDP	539	**Cyrus of Persia returns Jews to Israel** **Prophets** Haggai, Zechariah, Ezra, Nehemiah, Isaiah III, Obadiah, Malachi, Joel
	332	**Alexander the Great conquers Israel** Israel ruled by Ptolemies (Greeks in Egypt) then by Seleucids (Greeks in Syria) **Wisdom Literature** Proverbs, Job, Ecclesiastes, Song of Songs, Wisdom
	167	**Maccabees revolt** Daniel written
	63	**Romans conquer Israel**
	4	**Birth of Christ**

DEBORAH

BACKGROUND:
DEBORAH

After the Exodus event, and the 40 years in the desert, the Hebrews finally entered into the promised land of Canaan and populated it. This post-Exodus era lasted about two hundred years from when the descendants of Abraham returned to and eventually occupied the Promised Land to the time when they had their first king, Saul. In this time before the orderly structure of the monarchy, life for the Israelites was basically one of political chaos, famine and warfare.

The "judges" referred to in the Bible were not elected or appointed in any planned way. Each one was a character who was raised up for his or her gifts during a time of emergency—usually to lead the Israelites against a threatening enemy. Between such battles, the judges retired from military leadership and the "normal" pattern of chaos often returned. In some ways, the times resembled the American "Wild West" before law and order arrived. As it says in Judges 21:25, "all the people did what was right in their own eyes." Without the infrastructure of law and authority, the Israelites were a small tribal nation not unlike those that surrounded them.

The one difference between the Hebrews and their neighbors was their Covenant with Yahweh. Their fortunes rose and fell in response to their faithfulness to the Covenant. In times of spiritual and moral strength, they remained independent and prospered. When they lost sight of their unique covenant relationship with Yahweh and "did evil in the sight of the Lord" (3:7, 4:1), they fell victim to the attacks of their enemies. This theme of relying on God alone and remaining faithful to the Covenant runs throughout the history of biblical Israel and seems to still be an acquired learning in the time of the judges. Whenever Israel fell into oppression at the hand of their enemies and called out to Yahweh, "the Lord raised up judges to deliver them from the power of their despoilers" (2:16).

Of the twelve judges mentioned in the Book of Judges, at least six of them exercised military leadership. Deborah is the only judge to combine all the various forms of leadership— religious, military, juridical, and poetic.

"At this time the prophetess Deborah, the wife of Lappidoth, was judging Israel" (4:4). The phrase, "wife of Lappidoth," can also be translated "woman of fire," a title that characterizes Deborah well. Whether Lappidoth was a husband or a description of Deborah's character, her most important relationship is not with a spouse but with Israel and with the commander she appoints. She is also called a "mother in Israel" (5:7) and clearly acts symbolically in that capacity.

Sitting in judgment, as she did, under Deborah's palm tree, she settled disputes among the people and, no doubt, reflected on underlying causes of their anguish. The land was oppressed by Sisera, general of Hazor, who "with his nine hundred iron chariots sorely oppressed the Israelites for twenty years" (4:3). In her role as judge in Israel, she is the one to respond when "the Israelites cried to the Lord" (4:3).

The story of Deborah is told in Judges 4:4-16 in narrative form and then in song in 5:1-31. The focus of our study is Deborah and so we'll focus primarily on those verses but we will visit briefly the interlude between those sections where Jael slays the fleeing Sisera.

DEBORAH'S PRAYER

At this time the prophetess Deborah, wife of Lappidoth, was judging Israel. She used to sit under Deborah's palm tree, situated between Ramah and Bethel in the mountain region of Ephraim, and there the Israelites came up to her for judgment.

As one of charismatic judges of Israel, Deborah exercised her gifts of good judgment, vision, compassion, and a heart for others. God raised her up in a time of trial to save the people of Israel. This "Woman of Fire" used her unique gifts to empower others and to lead with courage.

Set our hearts aflame, O God of Deborah,

that we might recognize your stirring within us.

Embolden us to use the gifts we've been given

to serve You and to love your people.

Lay our ears upon the hearts of those who bless us with their stories.

Season our words with the salt of your wisdom.

Weave with us a partnership that empowers the powerless.

Fan the spark of passion into purifying flame.

Steady our hands and feet to act with courage.

Brighten our vision to focus always on your purpose in our lives.

Give us grateful hearts at the end

that we might praise you with joy and song.

Amen.

- KMcK

NEVER ON SUNDAY
A Look at the Women NOT in the Lectionary

WEEK TWO - DEBORAH

Judges: 4-5

1) *Deborah sat under a palm tree to listen to people's problems and render judgment. This is a different model than the judge Samuel who rode out on a circuit to hear cases (1 Sam7:16). How important is creating a space to listening? Where is your space for listening for God's wisdom, receiving other people's stories, discerning and judgment?*

2) *In listening to the needs of her people, Deborah saw beyond the seemingly unrelated complaints to the deeper causes. She recognized the oppression that created the distress. Can you think of someone who has the gift of listening deeply—in your own life or a public person? What difference has this person made? How good are you at identifying the deeper issues?*

3) *Deborah responded to God's call by building relationships. She did not think she had to do it all but, rather, built a partnership with Barak and a coalition of 10,000 troops. She showed both her willingness to share power and her willingness to lay her own self on the line. Can you think of others who have used their power and influence this way? What is the result? How have you done that in your own life? Is there any relationship-building that God is calling you to?*

4) *In building her coalition, Deborah showed a talent for matching the right person with the right gift. How does someone come by this ability to recognize the gifts of others?*

5) *"The war was at their gates" (5:8) and the roads had become unsafe (5:6). Deborah called herself a "mother in Israel" (5:7). Here we have an image of mother as leader and protector. When do think mothers show their stronger, more protective side? Why? Think of examples.*

6) *Many women have fought passionately to provide a better future, a freer society for their children. Can you think of any? What issues do you care passionately about? How have you acted on your passion?*

7) *Deborah did not engage in physical battle but was the instigator, planner, encourager, final decision-maker and was on-the-scene. What do you think of the role of woman warrior?*

8) *When Deborah led her people in a victory celebration she gave God the credit for the victory and she sang the praises of Barak and all the tribes who joined in the battle. How important is praise? In your relationship with God? With family, friends, co-workers?*

9) *The episode where Jael slays Sisera is troubling in its violence, deceit and surprising turn of gender roles. What do you think were her motives? The Bible is, at times, a violent book. What is your response to such episodes in the Bible?*

10) *Identify some of the qualities in Deborah. Which ones do you most admire? How are you like her? How would you like to be like her?*

11) *Choose to create a Midrash on the story of Deborah—as "wife of Lappidoth," sitting under the palm tree, beseeching Barak, singing and dancing with tambourine, or…? This can be a story, a poem, a picture…*

CHALLENGE

Google and read the poem, *Our Deepest Fear* by Marianne Williamson. Think deeply about your own leadership abilities. Identify the strengths you share with Deborah, your ability to: listen deeply to God and others, see the overall pattern of things, work with others and build partnerships, keep sight of the vision, have passion and conviction, willingness to put yourself on the line. Be brave enough to claim your strengths. Ask God who best to use them.

A CLOSER LOOK AT THE TEXT:
DEBORAH

Similar to Miriam's Song of the Sea, we have in Judges 5, the Canticle of Deborah. Like the Song of the Sea, it is the more ancient version of a story told elsewhere—in this case, Judges 4, and is a particularly good example of early Hebrew poetry. First comes the invitation, in vs. 1-3, to all the chiefs of Israel to bless the Lord. God's saving actions are underscored and magnified poetically in vs. 4-5, as would be the main purpose of the composer. The scene is set in vs. 6-7 of the travails throughout the land and the heroine Deborah, a mother in Israel, arises. Her response, and Barak's, is recounted in vs. 8-12 and the enlistment of the various tribes of Israel follows, vs. 12-18. The battle is told in vs. 19-23 and particularly colorful imagery in vs. 20-22 describes an apparent sudden storm that mires the chariots of Sisera in the mud. This allows the forces of Israel to attack and overcome their enemy much like the Egyptians of the Exodus were overcome by the collapsing walls of the Red Sea. A blessing and a curse follow, in typical Hebrew fashion, in vs. 23 and 24. Those tribes who did not come to the aid of the nation are cursed and Jael, the tent-dwelling woman, or nomad, is blessed. Verses 25-31 delight in the details of Sisera's downfall and even imagine the mother of Sisera awaiting a return that will never be. Pretty dramatic stuff! One can almost imagine the colorful, swirling dance that would accompany this song's being sung down the years.

As the older of the two texts, the details in the Canticle of Deborah that are at variance with Judges 4 are believed to be the more accurate. Thus, the description of Sisera's murder in 4:18-21 wherein he is slain in his sleep, is a later rendition. In 5:25-27, Jael strikes Sisera from behind as he drains a heavy bowl of curdled milk and he falls at her feet. It is intriguing to consider why later story-tellers altered the details. Was it some confusion or conflating with the story of Judith killing Holfernes (one we'll encounter later)? Why would elements of deceit and implied seduction be added? Are these considered "feminine" attributes that are somehow necessary to the story? Does is matter that Jael attacked a standing man who came, uninvited to her tent, as opposed to a sleeping man she'd invited in and duped?

While the focus of this week's study is Deborah, the inclusion in the story of Jael and Sisera cannot be overlooked and introduces the challenging, troubling topic of violence in the Bible. Violence in the Bible is doubling disturbing in that women are frequently the victims and in that rare exception when women are violent, as with Jael, it is seen as a reversal of the dominate roles. As Deborah warns Barak, "You shall not gain the glory in the expedition on which you are setting out, for the Lord will have Sisera fall into the power of a woman" (4:9). Just four chapters later in Judges, the wicked Abimelech is justly "requited for his evil" (9:56) when a woman casts a millstone upon his head. "He immediately called for his armor-bearer and said to him, 'Draw your sword and dispatch me, lest they say of me that a woman killed me.' So his attendant ran him through and he died" (9:54).

Most of us can recall biblical episodes that would not make good bedtime stories for children. The sacrifice of Abraham, though averted, is still chilling. Unfortunately, the daughter of Jephthah is not spared, nor is Lot's wife, the residents of Sodom, or the infants of Bethlehem. These are not even battle scenes. In creating the lectionary, one of the consequences is a "sanitized" collection. Many, though not all, of the violent scenes have been edited out. Take, for example, Psalm 137. Some of us will find it familiar from the musical Godspell that put portions of it to music, "By the streams of Babylon we sat and wept when we remembered Zion" (Ps 137:1). Or we have been struck by the longing and vivid imagery of "on the aspens of that land we hung up our harps, though there our captors asked of us the lyrics of our songs…How could we sing a song of the Lord in a foreign land?" Few of us have, however, read on to the closing lines, "O daughter of Babylon, you destroyer, happy the man who shall repay you the evil you have done us! Happy the man who shall seize and smash your little ones against the rock!" (Ps 137:8-9). Even the Church's Liturgy of the Hours, which is designed to incorporate all 150 psalms, omits this vicious passage.

It is good to recall that we are dealing here with an ancient text and the sensibilities that we bring to it were not shared by the people who lived and recorded the events in the pages. The Israelites and their writings are not unlike the other ancient people and texts of their era. We are no less responsible, however, to be honest about the fact that this violence exists in the pages of our most sacred book. We need also to be aware that such violence can affect our image(s) of God and, left unchallenged, can distort that image and, subsequently, adversely affect our own spirituality. We find ourselves asking questions like, "what kind of God condones or commands such violence?" Are we, including the biblical author, casting a God in human terms—creating God in our image, as it were, instead of God creating us in God's image?

We need to be very careful about how we appropriate scripture to ourselves. While the questions we ask in our reflection are helpful to instruct and inspire us, we need also to bear in mind that readers of scripture can find justification for most anything within the pages of the Bible. Consider, for example, that Jesus is quoted in Matthew, "He who is not with me is against me" (Mt 12:30) and in Mark, "Anyone who is not against us is with us" (Mk 9:40). One excludes; one includes. Both are quoted for the purposes of the one quoting. Context sometimes provides clarity and congruency but often does not. The text can be at odds with itself and contain inherent problems.

The Bible can be, and is, a dangerous text. It is dangerous because its message subverts unjust authority, breathes life and hope into those oppressed, gives God's people a vision of a different, better life and points to a Kingdom at odds with any kingdom yet seen on earth. It is also dangerous because it contains messages that can be, and are, used to further oppress, victimize and diminish humanity and all God's creation—even if that is done subconsciously.

Perhaps one of the takeaways from this consideration is how perilous it is to be too literal in applying scripture. There is too much in our sacred pages that cannot be taken as it appears. If nothing else, it should prevent us from casting judgment on the texts of other religions that also contain perilous texts amid the wisdom offered.

MEANWHILE, ON SUNDAY MORNING....

The prophets Gideon, Jotham, and Jepthah from the Book of Judges are included in the weekday lectionary but no mention of **Deborah** is made in either the Sunday or Weekday readings. Her canticle, believed by scholars to be one of the most ancient, intact examples of Hebrew poetry existent, is not included.

RUTH
AND
NAOMI

BACKGROUND:
RUTH AND NAOMI

The Book of Ruth, just four chapters in length, occurs right after the Book of Judges and is set in the same time period. Though, as we noted in the study of Deborah, these were chaotic times, they were not without standards in place. In addition to the Mosaic Law as received on Mt. Sinai during the Exodus, the Israelite community had a primitive code that governed their actions. We see this evidenced in the custom of gleaning—allowing the poor, the widowed and the stranger to follow the harvesters. Care and regard for the widow, orphan and stranger was an imperative from the earliest stages of Judaism. The levirate law is also referred to in the Book of Ruth, although its application to Ruth, as a Moabite, is, to say the least, exceptional. Levirate law allowed a widow the right to children by mating with her deceased husband's brother.

Naomi is aware of the laws of the land and has Ruth use them to advantage to gain security. We even see a curious remnant of prevailing custom in 4:7 where the taking off of one sandal and giving it to another sealed the contract between the two. This also verifies that the story was recorded after the fact in its phrasing, "Now it used to be the custom in Israel…"

Because there were no government structures in place during the time of the judges, when famine struck there was no help available, not even a king to whom one could appeal. Thus it fell to Elimech, the husband of Naomi, to make a difficult choice. Just as Jacob left the Promised Land in a time of famine, so Elimech, Naomi, and their two sons left Bethlehem of Judah for the plateau of Moab where they hoped economic conditions would be better. It was not an easy thing to leave the land God had promised to Abraham. This was not only the land of their ancestors, the patriarchs, it was also the land for which they endured forty years in the desert and then fought to regain.

The plight of the family was not unlike that of immigrants anywhere. Forced to leave what they knew and loved, they were in a strange land and the hoped-for good fortune did not occur. Some time after their arrival, Emilech died. In the ensuing ten years, Naomi watched her sons take Moabite wives but then both the sons died without having had children. Naomi was left without husband, sons or heirs. The dying out of the family line was the greatest of evils to befall Naomi. The value and role of a woman was to produce children and ensure the continuation of the family line. The levirate law, based on Dt 25:5-10, addressed such situations but Since Naomi had no other sons and was too old to bear more, it did not seem to offer hope in this case. There was no way to continue the family line.

Naomi was now a widow. *Va-tisher*, the Hebrew word for widow, means, literally, the "left-over" or the "husk." The term aptly described Naomi's condition. She was alone and without any means to raise up heirs or to care for herself. Her only remaining connection was her two Moabite daughters-in-law, Orpah and Ruth, themselves widows but widows still within the child-bearing years.

Naomi shows strength of character, however, in her ability to move on in the midst of loss. Leaving the Promised Land was her husband's decision but returning was hers. She hears that food is available there once again and resolves to return.

Because Orpah and Ruth are young enough, they would normally return home to their parents so that another marriage could be arranged for them. Something inspired them instead to set out with Naomi on the four to five day journey across the Jordan River and desert of Judah. Not only are they leaving what they know and taking on a perilous journey, they are entering "enemy" territory. The Moabites are the only people in scripture that the Torah condemns. There is little chance in Israel that they would be welcomed and almost none that they would have the opportunity to marry again.

Naomi knows what awaits the young women and clearly wants the best for them. The scene where they divide is particularly touching. She tries to send them back home with encouragement to have a husband and home. She kisses them good-bye and cries with loud sobs. Both of them protest they will not leave her for the bond of affection is obviously mutual. Naomi urges them further and, finally, Orpah kisses her and leaves in tears. Her decision, though painful, is a sensible and good one. All the more remarkable, then, is Ruth's decision to stay. Her words strike to the heart of a love relationship, "Do not ask me to abandon or forsake you! For wherever you go I will go, wherever you lodge I will lodge, your people will be my people, and your God my God" (1:16-17).

Once Naomi returns to Bethlehem, she again shows her concern for Ruth and her gentle wisdom in guiding her in actions that secure a future. In the end, the focus returns again to Naomi when the newborn son of Ruth and Boaz is placed upon Naomi's lap.

We have no information about the author of the Book of Ruth. Some scholars have suggested that it was originally a story told by women for other women. We have no way to verify the authorship. But this is a remarkable book in that the Bible is overwhelmingly about men, told from the point of view of men. Most of the time, women are mentioned only as they relate to the men in the story. This situation is completely reversed in the Book of Ruth. The main characters are women and the main theme is their relationship with one another. The men are mentioned only because of their relationship to the two women. As often as the theme of journey shows up in scripture, it is the journey of men—Abraham, Jacob, Joseph, etc. Here the journey is that of two women. Enjoy.

PRAYER OF
RUTH AND NAOMI

But Ruth said, "Do not press me to leave you and to stop going with you for wherever you go, I shall go, wherever you live, I shall live. Your people will be my people, and your God will be my God. Where you die, I shall die and there I shall be buried. Let Yahweh bring unnameable ills on me and worse ills, too, if anything but death should part me from you." (Ruth 1:16-17)

Ruth, the Moabite, teaches Israel what true faithfulness and love is and can be. She and Naomi model a cooperative venture of women helping each other, of generations helping each other. Ruth and Naomi conspire together for a future of hope. Ruth hands her life over to God and lives out her promise with exemplary faithfulness. Naomi gives her the freedom, the wisdom and the encouragement to do that. Together they are the first in scripture to show a preferential option for the poor and they give us a model for true intimacy. In so doing, they are an image of God's unfailing love.

Show us your loving-kindness, O God of Ruth and Naomi.

May we recognize your compassionate heart and, emboldened by your love for us, extend that kind of love to others:

to those closest to us who share our lives—may we be constant and kind in our care for them;

to those with whom we share our human struggles—may we uplift and sustain them by our solidarity and support.

We thank you for the example of others who have loved heroically and compassionately and we ask you to bless them for their goodness.

As we ourselves age, we ask that you help us to use the experience and wisdom of our years to think creatively and act boldly to bring about your justice.

May our gift to the next generation be a better world, a world that will receive their gifts with joy.

Amen.

- KMcK

NEVER ON SUNDAY
A Look at the Women NOT in the Lectionary

WEEK THREE - RUTH AND NAOMI

Book of Ruth

1) Naomi has "nothing left to lose" and so returns to Bethlehem. What wisdom, comfort, hope, promise does the familiar or past have to offer? Is there a freedom in nothing left to lose? Have you ever experienced being in a place like Naomi? What caused you to move?

2) Ruth says, "Your God shall be my God too." How have you relied upon the faith of others? When have you known others to rely upon your faith? When do you think in the story Ruth may have made Naomi's God her own? How did you transition from the faith of your parents or others to your own faith?

3) Despite her age, poverty and social standing, Naomi shows initiative—both in deciding to return to her homeland and in the advice she gives to Ruth. How does Naomi, seemingly powerless, have power? How does she use it? Think of other similar examples of those without strength who cause change.

4) As a widow, Naomi was a "va-tishir" or "left-over." She and Ruth stayed alive by the gleanings of Ruth. What leftovers—material or spiritual, have been valuable to you in our life? Isaiah 55 11 speaks of God's Word, "It shall not return to me void, but shall do my will, achieving the end for which I sent it." How does this speak to nothing being wasted to God's purpose? How does it speak to our disposable, consumerist society? How can we better honor gleaning in our lives?

5. *Have you ever experienced a generational connection with another woman that impacted your life in ways that brought about hope and possibility? Share her with your group.*

6. *Faithfulness is an enduring theme in Ruth. Naomi remembers and returns to the land, people and culture/faith of her past. Ruth pledges her faithfulness to Naomi and to Naomi's God. Boaz is the model of faithful leadership. And God is faithful, blessing them all abundantly at the end. What models of faithfulness speak to you and do you identify with? To what do you try to remain faithful? What rewards and struggles has that entailed? Why have you endured?*

7. *The same women who received Naomi as "Mara" surround her at the end, restored to well-being. Who has been community for you when you were "Mara" (bitter)? When you were "Naomi" (pleasant)? What difference has community made?*

8. *The closing scene of Ruth is truly a "happy ending." When have you had an event that caused you to proclaim, "Blessed be the Lord!"*

9. *With which woman do you find yourself identifying, Ruth or Naomi? Why? As always, you are invited to create a Midrash as that woman.*

CHALLENGE IF YOU IDENTIFY WITH RUTH

Ruth's example of *"hesed"*—loving-kindness, toward Naomi sets a high standard to follow. Who, in your life, has elicited that kind of loving compassion from you? Who has that kind of claim on your heart? Consider how to concretely convey *"hesed"* to that person. Write down the words you want to speak and the action you plan to do. Ask God for an opportunity to follow through.

CHALLENGE IF YOU IDENTIFY WITH NAOMI

Naomi made it possible for her daughter-in-law to have a future and to bring new life into being. What better world do you hope for the next generation—your own family and all humankind? Can you imagine one concrete step to help bring that about? Reflect, pray, and write out a personal goal to help make that happen.

A CLOSER LOOK AT THE TEXT:
RUTH AND NAOMI

The story of Ruth and Naomi exists like a novella within the larger context of scripture. It is engaging and inspiring to read but if it is only a lovely story, it begs the question, why was it included in the bible? It is, in fact, much more than enjoyable story for in the portrait of these two women and their relationship, Israel is given concrete example of what covenant love looks like. That example comes from a surprising source—a widow and a Moabite.

Together these two women pledge themselves to one another in selfless love and together they create a future that, alone, they did not have. That promise is beautifully vowed in Ruth's promise, "Wherever you go, I shall go, wherever you live, I shall live. Your people will be my people, and your God will be my God. Where you die, I shall die and there I shall be buried" (1:16-17). There is no finer articulation of *hesed*—the Hebrew word for loving-kindness, in all of scripture.

Like Mary's *fiat*, Ruth's pledge is unconditional and irrevocable even as it is completely without assurances about the future. And like Mary, Ruth lives out her commitment with remarkable faithfulness. In staying with the widow Naomi, Ruth gives over her life to God and throws her lot in with the poor and disenfranchised. Ruth takes that future on for herself even though she had the option of staying in Moab and remarrying.

The book of Ruth begins and ends with Naomi. She is similarly selfless in her willingness to urge both her daughters-in-law to a better life and once returned to Bethlehem she uses all the wisdom and resources at her command to assist Ruth. Together Naomi and Ruth *conspire*, "breathe together" to build a future that holds the promise of new life. That new life is realized in Obed who will become the father of Jesse, the father of David from whose line the Christ will come. Thus, the Moabite woman becomes the great grandmother of Israel's greatest king and part of the lineage of Jesus.

RUTH AND THE FEAST OF SHAVOUT

In most Christian Bibles, the Book of Ruth comes after Judges because the Septuagint or Greek translation of the Hebrew Bible placed it there. In the Jewish Canon, however, Ruth is included among the *Ketumin*, or "Writings." It is traditionally read on *Shavuot*, or Festival of Weeks, also known as Pentecost, coming 50 days after Passover. There is no correlation with this Jewish Feast of Pentecost to the Christian Feast of Pentecost, except that they each fall 50 days after their relative feasts of Passover and Easter and these are dated close to one another.

Shavout commemorates the anniversary of the day God gave the Torah to the Israelites at Mt. Sinai. It is specific in celebrating God's *giving* the Law, rather than Israel's *receiving* the Law for the first happened once in an historical time and place whereas the second is a timeless, ongoing engagement for all places and peoples. We can never say we have received, lived or fully understood the Covenant; that relationship is always a work in progress. The Law was given in the desert, the land outside of Israel, the Jewish homeland-to-be. This, too, underscores the universality of the gift that is the Law. Israel would go on to encode the living out of the basic Decalogue with numerous laws and code in the scriptures. But the 172 words that are the Ten Commandments define not only God's covenant relationship with historical Israel; they describe right relationship between all humanity and our Creator.

There is great complimentarity to the two feasts of Passover and Shavout. Where Passover celebrates the Exodus and freedom from physical slavery, Shavout celebrates the freedom from mental and spiritual slavery, freedom that comes from observing Torah. There is also completion with Shavout for it teaches that freedom comes with responsibility. The Law completed the saving action of the Exodus experience for it gave meaning and purpose to the freedom of God's people. They were not saved only for the purpose of being free. They were saved to enter into a new, covenanted relationship with God, a relationship that was defined by the Law given at Mt. Sinai.

It is customary to count the days in anticipation the days from Passover to Shavout, "Counting Omer." Omer is a measure of barley as in a sheaf and the counting is in keeping with the directive from Leviticus 23:15-16, "Beginning with the day after the sabbath, the day on which you bring the wave-offering sheaf, you shall count seven full weeks, and then on the day after the seventh week, the fiftieth day, you shall present the new cereal offering to the Lord." Shavuot is also connected to the season of the grain harvest, a seven week period that begins with the barley harvest at Passover and ends with the wheat harvest at Shavuot. During the time of the Jerusalem temple, it was customary to make two loaves of bread from the wheat harvest for offering. Today traditional foods associated with Shavuot are dairy and cheese. This may come from the anticipated entry into the "land flowing with milk and honey," or from the dietary restrictions that came with the law and that separated meat from dairy. At any rate, it has led to such Jewish delicacies as cheese blintzes and cheesecake.

Shavout is one of three pilgrimage feasts as proscribed in Dt 16:16, "Three times a year, then, every male among you shall appear before the Lord, your God, in the place which he chooses: at the feast of Unleavened Bread, at the feast of Weeks, and at the feast of Booths. No one shall appeear before the Lord empty-handed, but each of you with as much as he can give, in proportion to the blessings which the Lord, your God, has bestowed on you." By late antiquity, in the Roman era, Jews by the thousands came from throughout the Mediterranean world for these feast days. It was to accommodate these numbers that Herod the Great built the vast courtyard to the Jerusalem temple. The number of pilgrims created a large commercial network for the raising of livestock to be sacrificed, banking to exchange the various currencies, and taverns and inns for lodging. Pilgrimages were an important part of the religious life of the community in the way that they reaffirmed one's commitment, strengthened identity with the community and reinforced the sanctity of Jerusalem and its temple. All of this ended, of course, with the fall of the temple. The pilgrimage aspect of Shavout is simply that of an interior disposition toward commitment, identity and holiness.

It was only after the fall of the Temple that Shavout began to take on the role of celebrating Torah in addition to being a harvest and pilgrimage festival as written out in the scriptures. Today sacrifice has been replaced by prayer and the harvest aspects are retained in the foods and in the story of Ruth. The reading of the Book of Ruth at Shavout is likely due to the story taking place during the barley harvest. Additionally, she is, of course, the great-grandmother to David who, according to tradition, was born and died on Shavout. But Ruth's joining the Jewish people underscores what it means to be Jewish and how that is intrinsically defined by the Torah. Ruth is seen as the paradigm for *tzeddek* or "righteous convert." For the sake of her new people and new God, she gave up all her former life, at great sacrifice to herself. She is a reminder, then, of the great value of the Torah, the way of life that is Judaism. Shavout is a two day festival and it is customary, in fact, to spend the whole first night of Shavout reading and studying God's great gift, the Torah.

MEANWHILE, ON SUNDAY MORNING....

The whole of the Book of Ruth merits no mention on Sundays but has two excerpts on weekday readings, Friday of the Twentieth Week in Ordinary Time, Year 1 (#423) and Saturday of the Twentieth Week in Ordinary Tim, Year 1 (#424). The first one is the famous "Wherever you go…" passage and the second is the passage that exalts Ruth for bearing a son for her husband Boaz.

HULDAH

BACKGROUND:
HULDAH

Miriam afforded us the opportunity to trace Israel's history back to the Exodus experience, the Covenant on Sinai, and the formation of the people in the desert before entering the Promised Land. The women of Judges: Deborah, Ruth and Naomi, all came from that early period of settlement when Israel was a tribal nation among other such nations in the land. All that changed with Saul as Israel became a monarchy. That monarchy was at its height under David but only lasted as a united kingdom through his son, Solomon. After that it was divided into the Northern Kingdom of Israel and the Southern Kingdom of Judah. The Books of Kings and the Books of Chronicles tell the stories of the various kings after that but also of how the people kept, or failed to keep, the Covenant. Always the fortune of Israel is tied to how faithful they are to Yahweh. Throughout this time, the prophets continue to call Israel and Judah back to the Covenant and the various Books of the Prophets focus on that theme.

The world of Huldah is much different from that of the other women studied. She is an urban dweller living in the "Second Quarter in Jerusalem," an area in front of the temple. The Hebrew word for this part of Jerusalem was "Mishneh," meaning "a place of repetition." This likely refers to the oral repetition that was part of learning in that time—a place where schools were. Coupled with Huldah's ability to read and make judgment about the book she is given to authenticate, we can surmise that she was an educated woman. We also know that she is married to Shallum, the keeper of the king's wardrobe. Whereas Deborah's description as "wife of Lappidoth" can be alternately translated as "woman of fire," the translation here assures us that Huldah is both prophet and wife.

Huldah lives in tumultuous times. King Josiah was put upon the throne at age 8 after his father, Amon, had been assassinated just two years into his reign by members of his own court. The discontent went farther back to his father, Manasseh, who ruled for fifty-five years, the longest of any king in either Judah or Israel's history. He was also seen in the Second Book of Kings as the worst king in the nation's history for all the false gods he introduced, allying himself with foreign powers, his consultation of magicians and astrologers, the murder of innocent people—even the sacrificing of one of his sons to a pagan deity. So, the stage was set for this eight-year-old king to follow in different footsteps under the tutelage, no doubt, of reformers.

One of Josiah's first reforming efforts was to repair the temple. He was in the eighteenth year of his reign, 622 B.C., when the work was begun and it is not long before the high priest Hilkiah brought out a book that had been found hidden somewhere in the temple and presents it to the king. This is the central conflict in the story of Huldah as she is called upon to authenticate the newly discovered book. Its message is a dangerous one for it condemns the current state of affairs, the fall away from the Covenant, and it predicts downfall and ruin. Huldah is put in a most tenuous position with many cross currents and much at stake. There is too much at stake to be political. She can only be faithful. In her role as a prophet, she can only seek to know what is truly the word of God. And, in her role as a prophet, she must speak that truth, popular or not. It is interesting to note that this event happened during the time of the prophet Jeremiah and yet it is Huldah to whom Josiah turns for verification.

HULDAH'S PRAYER

So Hildiah the priest, Ahikam, Achbor, Shaphn, and Asaiah betook themselves to the Second Quarter in Jerusalem, where the prophetess Huldah resided. She was the wife of Shallum, son of Tikvah, son of Harhas, keeper of the wardrobe. When they had spoken to her, she said to them, "Thus says the Lord, the God of Israel…"

Whisper to our hearts, God of Huldah,

that we might know your will in our lives.

Give us the wisdom to know what is truly of You and what is not.

Give us patience to wait upon your word,

and a burning desire to follow your word.

Give us, also, the courage and conviction

to speak the truth your word reveals.

We thank you for the gift of your scriptures.

May we find there your truth; may we find You.

- KMcK

NEVER ON SUNDAY
A Look at the Women NOT in the Lectionary

WEEK FOUR - HULDAH

2 Kings 22:1-20, 23:1-3, 21-23, 2 Chronicles 34:1-33

1) *Huldah is called upon to authenticate the word of God. What characteristics must she possess to be able to recognize the truth?*

2) *Four times Huldah says, "Thus says the Lord, the God of Israel,…" From where does she draw her authority?*

3) *How do you discern what is God's will for you in your life? What practices, characteristics or resources help you?*

4) *Can you think of a time when you confused what YOU wanted for what God wanted for you? How did that happen? How can you prevent that from happening again?*

5) *Can you think of a time when God's will was very clear? When it surprised you? How did you know? What were the consequences?*

6) *Huldah is a prophetess to whom others, including the king, go. To whom do you go to help you sort out your spiritual questions? What advantage, if any, is there in having some other person in your life for this?*

7) *How important is the Bible to you in your spiritual life? How do you discover God's meaning in the scriptures?*

8) *What makes for true worship? How important is the ritual? How important is the attitude? How do you feel when you hear conflicting answers to that question?*

9) *Huldah is, like many of us, a married woman, an educated suburbanite with a heart for God and a deep concern for her community of faith. She is also a prophetess. How do these two images strike you? Do they contradict, compliment or co-exist? Are there similar prophets in our own time? How might you be called upon by God to use your gifts as Huldah did?*

CHALLENGE

Huldah had a keen gift of discernment, the ability or understanding to separate truth from error. Test yourself on your ability to learn this from life. Make two columns on a piece of paper. At the top or one write, "I used to think..." At the top of the other write, "Now I know..." Number from one to ten down the side and fill in. Note what things have been reversed and what has been confirmed. Write a prayer of thanksgiving to God for what you have learned and ask for the guidance to continue to grow.

A CLOSER LOOK AT THE TEXT:
HULDAH

What is this "book of the law" that is found in the story of Huldah? Scholars believe that it was some form of the Book of Deuteronomy, probably the middle sections, Chapters 4 through 28. The form that this book takes is that of a single speech by Moses given on the banks of the Jordan just before the people are to cross over and begin to conquer the Promised Land. Of the five books of the Pentateuch, it is singularly different in its style and its language. Since the 18th century, scripture scholars have known that Deuteronomy dates from a much later time than these other books. It is framed as being Moses' last will and testament, his farewell speech to the people, and favors an oratory style that continually urges obedience to the law. By using this setting, the authors of Deuteronomy effectively convey the message in the true tradition of Moses. This method of writing was very common in the ancient world as a way of linking a teaching to its real and ancient source, thus giving it added authority.

The word Deuteronomy (deutero + nomos, in Greek) means "second law" and its law code, chapters 12-26, is similar to the covenant law of Exodus 20-23. Its language and specifics reflect, however, its later composition. For example, Ex. 23:10-11 commands farmers to leave the land fallow every seventh year so that the poor can survive off the wild re-grown grain. In Deuteronomy 15:1-11, however, extensive regulations are added for forgiving the debts owed by the poor and to regulate foreign borrowing and lending—the kinds of issues that would only arise in a more settled time and economy.

As we learned in the earlier study, *Sisters in Scripture*, much of the Pentateuch can be sorted out as originating from either of two originally oral traditions—the **Yahwist, known as "J,"** and the **Elohist, known as "E."** These terms derive from the name each tradition typically used for the Divine—"Yahweh," usually translated as God, or "Elohim," usually rendered as Lord. Scholars explain the bringing together of these two sources as well as this **"D,"** or **Deuteronomist** portion and the later **"P" Priestly** portion in something called The Wellhausen Document Theory. *A copy of that is in the back of the book under "Resources."* It was most likely around 720 to 700 B.C., in the reign of King Hezekiah of Judah that the **"J"** and **"E"** sources were combined to form the Books of **Genesis, Exodus, Leviticus** and **Numbers**. It was also under Hezekiah that the central chapters of **Deuteronomy** were written as the basis of a reform much like that of Josiah one hundred years later. The son of Hezekiah, Manasseh, reversed his father's reform and, in fact, began an age of persecution. It is believed that the "book of reform" was hidden away in the temple or simply lost or forgotten. It is also quite likely that it was protected by priests or Levites until a time should come when it was safe to bring it out of hiding. That time came in the reign of King Josiah. Once Josiah confirmed through the prophetess Huldah that it was authentic, it had a profound effect on the king and the kingdom.

By reading 2 Kgs. 23, we can glimpse not only how sweeping were Josiah's reforms but how far Israel had strayed from the Covenant code. All of these had to be done away with: idols to Baal and Asherah within the temple, cultic prostitution in the temple, places of worship to other gods in outlying areas, and the consultation of ghosts and spirits. We also see that the celebration of Passover was restored. "The king issued a command to all the people to observe the Passover of the Lord, their God, as it was prescribed in that book of the covenant" (vs 21). No Passover such as this had been observed during the period when the judges ruled Israel, or during the entire period of the kings of Israel and the kings of Judah, until the eighteenth year of King Josiah, when this Passover of the Lord was kept in Jerusalem.

It is hard to imagine a Judaism that had no Passover and that had so seriously lost its identity in the pursuit of other gods. Without the reforms of Josiah, undertaken at the urging of the prophetess Huldah, one wonders if the Covenant would have survived.

A WORD ABOUT THE DUPLICATE STORIES IN 1 & 2 KINGS AND 1 & 2 CHRONICLES: *see chart, page 25.*

It was toward the end of the monarchy that the Historical Books: Joshua, Judges, 1 & 3 Samuel, 1 & 2 Kings, were written down. Note that while Ruth is grouped with these books in the Bible because of its setting, it was written at a later time. These Historical Books tell the story of the conquest and settling of the Promised Land, of the growing need for a monarchy and, then, the story of that monarchy. They are of a similar writing style to that of the Book of Deuteronomy, as well as period of time, and, thus, they are also attributed to **"D,"** the **Deuteronomic** author.

1 & 2 Chronicles also tells the story of Israel's history but this time it is told from the perspective of **"P,"** the **priestly** writer. These books date to the time after the Babylonian Exile. While the events covered in 1&2 Chronicles are often the same events described in 1&2 Kings, the style, the purpose and the emphasis are different—not different enough to show up in our Huldah selections but different overall.

MEANWHILE, ON SUNDAY MORNING....

Huldah suffers the same fate as Shiphrah and Puah. Her story is told in a weekday reading, Wednesday of the Twelfth Week of Ordinary Time, Year II (#373) but she is edited out of the telling. The selection that is chosen for that day is 2 Kings 22:8-13, 23:1-3. The verses that refer to Huldah, (15-19), are neatly cut out.

ESTHER

BACKGROUND:
ESTHER

The setting for the Book of Esther is in the period under King Xerxes, who ruled from 486 to 465 B.C. The Jews went to Babylon in exile in 587 when Jerusalem was destroyed. Cyrus of Persia later overthrew the Babylonians and allowed the Jews to return to Israel. Many, however, remained in the lands to which they'd been exiled. The Jews in this story are living in exile in Susa, a city in Persia, about 650 miles northeast of Jerusalem. They are an oppressed people under the rule of Xerxes, referred to as Ahasuerus, and grandson of Cyrus. After Ahasuerus divorces his queen in a fit of rage, he sends out an edict searching for virgins to join his harem that he might find one who can become the next queen. No doubt Esther was one of those rounded up for the harem without any ability to choose otherwise. Through the influence of Mordecai, Esther's uncle, and several plot twists that the story skillfully lays out, the beautiful young Jewish maiden, Esther, rises to the position of queen. When Mordecai clashes with the evil Persian Prime Minister, Haman, the king is tricked by Haman into issuing a decree to slaughter all Jews of the land on a specific date. Esther consults with Mordecai, prays, fasts, and then bravely reveals Haman's trickery and her own Jewish identity. She wins the king over, tragedy is averted, the roles are reversed and the Jews end up slaughtering their enemies instead.

This exciting tale of intrigue and escape from mortal danger provides the basis for the Jewish feast of Purim. As such, an actual historical incident most likely is the basis for the story. That incident was probably a smaller, more local one but as the story was celebrated in prayer, story and song over the years, it became elevated to the level of its present setting within the royal household of Persia.

In the story, King Ahasuerus is an absolute ruler with power over life and death. He banishes and divorces the beautiful Queen Vashti for refusing to be put on display for his drunken guests. No one was allowed to approach him unless he raised his golden scepter and granted permission. Otherwise, they would be killed. The historical Xerxes shared these traits with the one in Esther's story. He unsuccessfully attacked the Greeks several times and, on one occasion, when a storm destroyed one of this troop's pontoon bridges, he ordered the soldiers to beat the waves with whips in punishment.

An important element of Persian law in this story is the immutable nature of a royal decree. Thus, when Vashti is banished, she cannot be recalled and when a date is set for the slaughter of the Jews it cannot be rescinded; it can only be superseded by another edict, the one allowing Jews to arm and defend themselves.

Notice in reading this story that it has a sophisticated plot with twists and turns and building suspense. Some characters like Haman, his wife Zeresh, and Ahasuerus are one dimensional prototypes but Esther and Mordecai are complex and their relationship evolves within the story.

ABOUT THE DIFFERENT TRANSLATIONS....

The Book of Esther will appear in two different forms depending on the translation of the Bible that you are using. In the New American Bible, Jerusalem Bible and other "Catholic" translations, those portions of Esther which come from the Greek are incorporated into the text—but you will notice how differently they are numbered, using letters to mark their inclusion. In the Revised Standard, New Revised Standard, New International or other "Protestant" translations, these same passages are separate from the Book itself and can be found in the Apocryphal portion of your Bible.

These differences are not actually differences in translation—the wording is essentially the same; they are differences in editing. The ten chapters of Esther as they exist in the Protestant canon, without the apocrypha, and the ten chapters of Esther as they exist in the Catholic canon, excluding the lettered portions—these are the passages that exist written only in Hebrew. The additional passages are ones that were written in Greek. These represent later additions to the Hebrew text. The canon of the Bible as first put together by the Catholic Church included some Greek sources. The later Reformers questioned the validity of these passages and chose only to include in their canon those writings that were in Hebrew—though they are now typically included as the Apocrypha in a separate section of the Bible. Thus, the following Books and portions of books appear only in Roman Catholic, Greek and Slavonic Bibles:

Tobit
Judith
Portions of Esther
Wisdom Sirach Baruch
The letter of Jeremiah (same as Baruch 6)
Portions of the Book of Daniel
1 Maccabees
2 Maccabees

Keep this in mind as you come together to share your reflections with the group. If you are using a Protestant canon, you will want to access the Apocrypha to have available to you the same passages that others in your group are reading. Because reflection questions draw from your own reaction to the text, it will be important to have all read the same materials. For now, be sure you all read the same thing and when we come together next time, we will learn more about how the differences occurred.

ESTHER'S PRAYER

Then Esther said in reply to Mordecai, "Go, gather all the Jews to be found in Susa, and hold a fast on my behalf, and neither eat nor drink for three days, night or day. I and my maids will also fast as you do. After that I will go to the king, though it is against the law; and if I perish, I perish." (4:15-16)

Give us courage, O God of Esther, to do what You call us to do.

Do not let us hide in the security of our own comfort, privilege or gender.

Help us remember our identity as one of your own; let us not be silent in the face of evil.

Unite us in spirit with others who are also your people.

Help us prepare our hearts that we might know when and how You would have us act, when and what You would have us speak.

May we use whatever power we have to give life to those without power.

Give us such confidence in You that we might place our lives in your hands.

Amen.

- KMcK

NEVER ON SUNDAY
A Look at the Women NOT in the Lectionary

WEEK FIVE - ESTHER

The Book of Esther

1)   *What do you think of Queen Vashti and the episode in 1:10-20? Was she foolish, vain, wise, proud, afraid, disdainful, other? What do you make of the reaction of the king and his aides? What do you think Ahasuerus "remembered" about Vashti (2:1) once his anger had abated?*

2)   *Both Vashti and Esther are beautiful but Esther does not fall from grace? Why? With whom do you identify? Why?*

3)   *Esther went from an orphan raised in Mordecai's home to the harem of the king to the Queen of Persia. Can you imagine a young girl going through such changes? She starts out with no power and rises to great, though carefully balanced, influence. When do you think she began to have some power? How does she find the wisdom to make the transition?*

4)   *What happens when those with great power isolate themselves from the people they rule? How corrupting do you believe power to be? Can you think of examples when it is not?*

5)   *When Mordecai first requests that Esther go to the king to "entreat him for her people" (4:8), Esther is reluctant and points out that to approach the king without summons means death. Where, with whom, are you least comfortable speaking up?*

6)   *Mordecai's response, vs. 13-14, persuades Esther to act. Why do you think Esther changed her mind? What part of his argument do you find the most compelling? What would it take for you to overcome such fear?*

7)   Esther aligns herself with the people for whom she is to intercede. What is the significance of the three days fast? How do you prepare, from whom do you seek assistance, when you are confronted with a difficult task?

8)   Look for all the places where time plays a role in this story. How important is it to know when to act and when to wait? Have you experienced waiting for the right moment to speak or act? How do you know the "right moment?" What was God doing while you are waiting?

9)   Once Esther realizes the situation, she intervenes—she steps in and alters the course of events. She is timely, persuasive and effective. There are such moments in the human story and in each of our stories. Can you think of others who have had to do as Esther did? When have you had to intervene to prevent disaster, to preserve life?

10) What qualities of Esther do you most admire? Which qualities do you identify with or wish you shared with her?

11) What do you think is the moral of the story of Esther?

CHALLENGE

Though the roles end up reversed in this story, Haman's planned annihilation of the Jews is mirrored many times in the pogroms of history up to Hitler's holocaust. "If you keep silence at such times..."(4:14), Mordecai's words are an indictment of complicity that we each need to consider. Re-read *Anne Frank's Diary*, rent *Schindler's List*, or go to the website for the United States Holocaust Memorial Museum, www.ushmm.org. Reflect, pray, ask God what you are being called to do in response.

A CLOSER LOOK AT THE TEXT:
ESTHER

The story of Esther is celebrated in Judaism by the Festival of Purim. The name Purim means "lots" (9:24) and refers to the lottery whereby Haman chose the date for the extermination of the Jews. That date was the 13th of Adar and, tables turned, the Jews triumphed instead on the next day. Purim falls on the 14th and 15th days of the Jewish month of Adar—usually in March (4:21). Because the Jewish calendar is lunar and our reckoning for Easter is also lunar, the festival of Purim and the Christian celebration of Easter are often close to one another. Ironically, Purim often falls near to the Christian observance of Good Friday, a day which, tragically, was the occasion for pogroms, particularly in 19th and early 20th C. Eastern Europe. It is on Good Friday that the narrative of Christ's death and passion is read and there have been times that the role of the Jews was preached upon and this led to violence against them. (See NOTE below).

The Feast of Purim is preceded by a minor fast recalling Esther's own fast of three days. The observation takes its direction directly from the lines of scripture: "they should make them days of feasting and gladness, days for sending gifts of food to one another and presents to the poor" (9:22). Purim is, therefore, a joyous feast. The Talmud, in fact, instructs people to drink until they cannot tell the difference between the words, "cursed by Haman" and "blessed be Mordecai." One of the special Purim foods is the *Hamantaschen* or "Haman's pocket," a fruit-filled triangular cookie that represents the three cornered hat that Haman wore. (*A recipe for Hamantaschen is in the Resources at the back of the book*). The sending out of food gifts to the poor, known as *shalach manos* is also a part of the Purim observation. The most important observance of Purim, however, is the reading of the Book of Esther. It is read, usually in the synagogue in the evening and again in the morning. This is referred to as the reading of the *Megillah* or scroll. There are five books in the Megillah—Esther, Ruth, Ecclesiastes, Song of Songs and Lamentations. The others may be read but Esther is always read. While the story of Esther is read, every time the name of Haman is said, listeners hiss and boo to blot out the name and memory of him. Noisemakers called *graggers* are also used. The noisemakers, food and drink have made this a truly fun, festive holiday. Sometimes masks and costumes are part of the observation and children especially love the holiday.

If we look at the Book of Esther as it exists in Hebrew, i.e. without those portions added from the Greek, one of the most astonishing things about it—and something we can miss if we read only from the Catholic canon, is that there is no mention of God in the Hebrew version. The Greek portions represent a later addition that include the lengthy prayers and may well have been a way to address this rather shocking oversight. The Book of Esther almost did not make it into the Jewish canon for this very reason. It did not achieve undisputed canonical status in Judaism until the third century. When the Church formed the canon a century later it followed the Jewish canon and included Esther but it also included the Greek additions. The most likely reason that Esther was included in the Jewish Canon was, in fact, the festival of Purim, which had become extremely popular and had been celebrated by the Diaspora Jews for many centuries— even before Judaism compiled its canon.

Both the setting and the audience of the Book of Esther are the Diaspora Jews. The Diaspora goes back to the Exile and the deportation of Jews from their homeland. Though they were later allowed to return under Cyrus of Persia, many remained in Babylon and migrated to other regions as well. This group of Jews who remained outside of Palestine became known as the Jewish Diaspora. The moral of Esther speaks especially to them as it encourages them not to lose their Jewish identity in an alien place. The Greek additions to the Hebrew in the Book of Esther most likely came from later Diaspora Jews who wrote in Greek. This also explains why the Greek language was used for the other biblical (or apocryphal) books that were authored after the Exile.

Another interesting item of note is that the Book of Esther is the only book not represented in the finds of the Dead Sea Scrolls. Scholars believe that the Qumran community that owned the scrolls would likely have disapproved of the book and, thus, did not have it in their library. The people living at Qumran were ascetics and would not have accepted the merry- making that had become a part of Purim. It is also a book that did not even mention the name of God in its Hebrew form, and in which the heroine does not keep kosher but, rather, lives and participates in a Gentile world. All of this would have been unacceptable to the ascetic community of Qumran.

MEANWHILE, ON SUNDAY MORNING....

The only selection from the Book of Esther which is chosen as a lectionary reading is her prayer for strength on a weekday in Lent (#228). There are three other passages from the Book of Esther that are found as optional readings in the Common of the Saints (#737) and the Masses for Various Occasions (#821, #876) but these might never be actually used in a parish. All three of these optional selections are accounts of the prayer of Mordecai, Esther's uncle, not Esther. Her actual story is never told or referred to at liturgy.

NOTE:

Pogrom is a Russian word meaning to "wreak havoc" and is a form of riot directed against a particular group. It usually included the destruction of homes, businesses and religious centers and instances of physical violence, even murder, against persons or groups of people. Pogrom became a common usage term in English with the large scale anti Jewish riots of 1881-1884 in SW Imperial Russia. A bloodier wave followed in 1903-1906 orchestrated by Orthodox priests and unofficially sanctioned by civil authorities. This led to widespread outcry and the eventual emigration of some 2 million Jews. Pogroms continued in the Russian Revolution and Civil War and spread in the 1920's to Poland, Romania and Argentina. Anti-Semitism, however, goes much farther back. Some examples of extreme anti-Semitism in history would include:

German Crusade of 1096

Expulsion of the Jews from England in 1290

Spanish Inquisition

Expulsion of the Jews from Spain in 1491

Expulsion of the Jews from Portugal in 1497

Various Pogroms in Europe

Hitler's Holocaust of the Jews in 1930's & 40's

JUDITH

BACKGROUND:
JUDITH

The opening lines of the Book of Judith appear to date it to a particular time frame but, in fact, are intended to alert the reader to its non-historical nature. Nebuchadnezzar was not the ruler of the Assyrians but of the Babylonians. The pairing of these two arch enemies of Israel—Assyria and Babylon, into one person and the scope of all that is described in the opening scenes of Judith introduces to the reader not an historical setting, but to a fictional one. It would be as if we read, "Abraham Lincoln crossed the Delaware River with his troops on Christmas Eve." It would be an obvious conflation of significant personages. We would understand that is was factually in error even as we understood that it was addressing something of great significance. In this case, the message conveyed by such a setting is that "all the world" is arrayed against Israel.

The first seven chapters set the scene for the conflict. Chapters one through four give details of Holofernes' conquest, confirming the power of Israel's enemy. In chapters five and six, the underlying premise for the story is articulated by Achior who is summoned before Holofernes. From the mouth of this Ammonite, a member of one of Israel's ancient Canaanite rivals, comes a summary of their history and the conclusion that the security of the Israelites depends entirely upon their fidelity to the Covenant with their God. "So now, my lord and master, if these people are at fault, and are sinning against their God, and if we verify this offense of theirs, then we shall be able to go up and conquer them. But if they are not a guilty nation, then your lordship would keep his distance; otherwise their Lord and God will shield them, and we shall become the laughing-stock of the whole world" (5:20-21). Of course, Holofernes, in his arrogance, rejects this advice, "What god is there beside Nebuchadnezzar?... Their God will not save them; but we, the servants of Nebuchadnezzar, will strike them down as one man, for they will be unable to withstand the force of our cavalry" (6:2-3). In chapter seven the siege begins. The Israelites are cut off from their water supply and surrounded for thirty-four days. They go to Uzziah and the leaders of the city pleading that peace be made with the Assyrians. Uzziah presses them to wait five more days for God to show his mercy toward them and then, after that, he will surrender if need be. At the close of this first section, the men take up their posts on the walls as the women and children return to their homes and all await disaster. The stage is set for a surprising turn of events.

Enter Judith. Her genealogy is the longest recorded of any woman in the whole of scripture and her attributes are immediately praise-worthy. Despite her being a woman and a widow to boot, the strengths of her character are impeccable. She unhesitatingly takes the initiative and offers a radically different theological perspective on the present situation. Uzziah acknowledges the wisdom of some of what she says and suggests, somewhat patronizingly, that she go home and pray. Judith sets the record straight that her intention is not to only pray but to act. "I am about to do something that will go down through all generations of our descendants" (8:32). Uzziah and the leaders cede all initiative to Judith, wish her well, and return to their former state of waiting.

The story of her triumph over Holofernes combines several of the attributes and themes of the women we have already seen. At the very end Judith, much like **Miriam**, leads the women of Israel in a dance that gives glory to God and that celebrates and commemorates the great victory. Like **Deborah**, she determines to act in the interests of her people even if it means stepping outside of the womanly realm and onto the battlefield. At the opportune time, she advises the forces of Israel how to seize their opportunity and gain the advantage. She conspires with her maid in a way that is reminiscent of the partnership of **Ruth and Naomi**. Like **Huldah**, she seems to know what it is God is asking of her; her plan seems to be clear in her mind from the beginning though she subsequently prays and prepares at great length. Her plan of action parallels that of **Esther** as she draws upon all her beauty, feminine wiles, and sexuality to gain access to great power. Lastly, in a scene much like **Jael**'s slaying of Sisera, Judith decapitates Holofernes—this time in his tent.

JUDITH'S PRAYER

"O God, my God, hear me also, a widow. It is you who were the author of those events and of what preceded and followed them. The present, also, and the future you have planned. Whatever you devise comes into being; the things you decide on come forward and say, 'Here we are!' All your ways are in readiness, and your judgment is made with foreknowledge" (Judith 9:5-6).

Give us confidence, O God of Judith, not that we are strong but that You are faithful.

Embolden us to act with determination against the evils of our day.

Do not let us retreat into passive indecision and relying upon others.

But, with clarity of purpose and firm reliance upon your aid,

let us use whatever power we possess to bring about your plan for ourselves and for your people.

Keep before us always the knowledge that You are the author of our lives and of all events.

Let us grow in our trust and confidence in You that we might recognize your purpose and rejoice in its fulfillment.

Amen.

- KMcK

NEVER ON SUNDAY
A Look at the Women NOT in the Lectionary

WEEK SIX - JUDITH

The Book of Judith

1) *What do you think is the underlying message of Judith? Why was this setting used for it?*

2) *Compare the despair and weakness of Israel's leaders with the confidence, trust and prayerfulness of this "helpless" widow. Wherein does true "power" reside? Discuss the meaning of power, the source of power. Can you think of any possibilities where those, seemingly without power, actually have power? What does this story say to similar "helpless" populations like the "widows" of our time?*

3) *Judith took exception to the leaders' promise to surrender if God did not intervene. Re-read 8:11-16. On what grounds does Judith object? What is her understanding of how God acts in our lives? Do you find wisdom there for your own prayer life?*

4) *It is clear from the onset, as soon as Judith appears on the scene, that she has a plan. Can you think of another person from your own life, or from history, who seems to have a clear direction from the get-go of what needs to be done, and the determination to do it? Where does this come from? How do you relate to such persons?*

5) *Judith is willing to put at risk her personal safety, her reputation, her virtue, and, possibly, her life for the sake of her people. For what would you be willing to risk it all?*

6) *As a woman, Judith uses the only weapons she has at her disposal. She has been both praised and criticized for using her feminine wiles as she does. How comfortable or uncomfortable are you with the choices she makes? Is she a role model? Why or why not?*

7) Can you think of a time when you did the "wrong" thing for an outcome that you believed to be good and more important?

8) Violence has been done in the name of God since the beginning of religious history. How can we reconcile that fact with the purpose and message of religion? Is it only zealots who do this? Is it possible there are situations when violence can/should be done in God's name?

9) Suggestion: Imagine you are Judith's maid and write a Midrash from that perspective.

CHALLENGE

Imagine a "Judith" with whom you can identify, e.g. a WWII member of the French underground helping with the Normandy invasion. Now imagine a "Judith" whom you see as misguided, e.g. a Muslim believer in Jihad. What are the differences? The similarities? The underlying issues? What can be done about them? Pray and journal on the thoughts and feelings that this brings out in you. Find someone with whom you can share these thoughts and questions.

A CLOSER LOOK AT THE TEXT:
JUDITH

The Book of Judith is the latest one written of all the books we have read—perhaps as late as 150 B.C., probably written within Palestine. Although the text exists only in the Greek, scholars agree that it is translated from an earlier Semetic, probably Hebrew, text that no longer exists. Judith never made it into the Hebrew Canon and, thus, its exception from the Protestant Canon. It is, however, adopted for reading at Hanukkah and Jerome mentions it in the 4th C. as being read in the Christian Church. The early Church chose to include it in the Canon in the 4th C. and, thus, its present inclusion in the Catholic Canon.

Judith is connected indirectly to the celebration of Hanukkah (see note). One tradition identifies her as Judith Maccabee, the daughter of Mattathias, the High Priest, and sister, therefore, to Judah Maccabee and the other four Maccabean sons. Her name is the feminine equivalent of Judah and in some Jewish circles, Hanukkah celebrates the two Jewish heroes together—Judah Maccabee and Judith. One of the traditional foods of Hanukkah is cheese latkes. Tradition says that Judith fed Holofernes salty cheese which made him so thirsty that he drank too much wine causing him to fall into a deep sleep. The cheese latkes commemorate Judith's food offering and are made in her honor.

Of all the women in scripture, Judith is the one most praised explicitly and profusely (Judith 8:7-8, 8:29, 13:18, 13:19, 15:9). She also acts independently of any male influence. There are no men in the Book of Judith who take a role in the deliverance that she brings about—no, Moses Barak, Boaz, Josiah or Mordecai. Judith alone, with the assistance of her handmaid, rescues her people from the hand of a foreign ruler.

In many ways Judith represents Israel by the time this book is written. Surrounded by larger, more powerful nations, Israel is, by contrast, as weak as a woman, a widow. She is not, however, powerless—if she remembers the Covenant and Yahweh's faithfulness. Relying on her God, Israel can expect that she will be delivered at great odds and in surprising ways. Faithfulness is the key and Judith exemplifies Israel at its best—prayerful, faithful, beautiful, brilliant, fearless, determined and pure. Judith's triumph is Israel's triumph and promised deliverance, a message of great hope in a time of peril.

We can justifiably celebrate that, with Judith, we have covered 12 centuries of Jewish history. We began with the seminal *Exodus* event and the prophetess **Miriam** who led her people in celebration at the Red Sea. Along with **Jochebed**, the **Pharaoh's daughter**, and the midwives, **Shiphrah** and **Puah**, she made it possible for Moses to survive and lead his people out of bondage. The *Period of Judges* followed and was an unsettled time but a time that called for the talents of a woman like **Deborah**—prophetess, warrior, mother in Israel, judge. She forged together an army that saved Israel from its enemy, an enemy that was slain at the hand of another woman, **Jael**. Judges is also the setting for the gentle, inspiring story of **Ruth** and **Naomi**. Together they taught the meaning of Covenant Love to Israel and still do to us today. Women did not rise to leadership in the *Period of the Monarchy* but after the fall of the Northern Kingdom at a time of great national need, the prophetess **Huldah** was called upon and predicted the *Exile* that soon followed. Though a remnant returned after the Exile, many Jews remained scattered outside of Palestine. The Book of **Esther** speaks to these *Diaspora* Jews and their struggle to maintain their identity and keep the Covenant. With **Judith** we come to a prototype of the Jewish predicament in the first two centuries before Christ. We are at the threshold of the Second Testament.

NOTE:

The Jewish Festival of Hanukkah celebrates the dedication of the Jerusalem Temple in 165 B.C. by Judah Maccabee after he and his followers, the Maccabeens had successfully overthrown the Seleucids. King Antiochus Epiphanes, IV, had conquered Palestine as part of the Greek Syrian kingdom, the Seleucids. In 168 B.C he outlawed the practice of Judaism and turned the Jewish temple into a Greek temple to Zeus. In the persecution of the Jews that followed, a Hasmonean High Priest named Mattathias and his five sons refused to submit. They went into hiding and began to attack using guerilla tactics. Mattathias was killed but his son, Judah, took over and others came to join them. Eventually the Maccabees prevailed. When Judah went to re-dedicate the temple he could find only enough pure olive oil in the temple to burn the lamp for one night. The lamp miraculously burned for all the eight nights of festivities.

That is the origin of the *menorah*, and *Hanukkah*, as the Festival of Lights. Each night an additional candle of the eight pronged menorah is lit and traditional blessings are prayed. Foods that accompany Hanukkah are those traditionally fried in oil to recall the miracle of the oil that lasted. Such treats include cheese latkes, potato latkes and *sufganiyot*, jelly-filled doughnuts. Playing with the *dreidle* at Hanukkah is said to go back to the persecution under the Seleucids when studying the Torah was forbidden. An outlook would be posted and if a soldier came near, the scroll would be hidden and, instead, a top would be spun to appear as if they were gambling. The Hebrew letters inscribed on the dreidel are an acronym for "A Great Thing Happened Here."

The successful revolt under Judah Maccabee led to the Hasmonean Jewish Kingdom which lasted from 166 BC until 63 BC when Rome invaded and conquered Palestine.

MEANWHILE, ON SUNDAY MORNING....

There are two short passages from the Book of Judith that are included as possible choices on weekdays. For feasts that use the Common of the Blessed Virgin (#709), "You are the highest honor of our race" (Judith 13:18, 19, 20) may be chosen for the Responsorial Psalm. For feasts that draw from the Common of the Saints, Judith 8:2-8) may be chosen (#737) praising Judith's asceticism and physical beauty. In each of these cases the attributes of Judith are used to underscore the virtues of another. Her story of saving the Israelites is told nowhere in the lectionary.

See **"RESOURCES"** for a recommended
DAY OF REFLCTION between these two Testaments

SECOND

OR

NEW TESTAMENT

MARY

IN UNEXPECTED PLACES

BACKGROUND:
MARY

As we move from women of the First Testament, or Hebrew Scriptures, to women of the Second Testament, or Christian Scriptures, it is important to remember that the women we will encounter in this second half are also Jewish women—except for a couple of Gentile converts to Christianity at the end of our study. Mary and all the women of the Gospels are Jewish women who stand in the footsteps of these other women we have studied. These earlier ones were known to the women we now encounter and share many qualities with them. Judith and Mary are separated by only a couple hundred years. Seen from this vantage point, the transition from the Old to the New Testament is a natural progression.

You will notice that this week's reading includes going back to 1 Samuel 1:1-2:11, the story of Hannah. This is largely because the Magnificat, Mary's song about conceiving Jesus, is a significant part of Mary's story that is not in the lectionary. Her words hearken back to the words of Hannah in the story of Samuel. When Hannah brings three-year-old Samuel to the temple to offer him to God she sings a song in thanksgiving for the son she was allowed to bear. Mary's song and Hannah's song are very similar. Mary is not quoting Hannah but her familiarity with her own tradition, its stories, and songs shines through in her own words. She was, no doubt, familiar with all the women we have studied and more. Notice how similar Mary's words are to those of Hannah.

HANNAH (1 Samuel 2)	MARY (Luke 1)
Hannah prayed and said, 'My heart exults in the LORD; my strength is exalted in my God. My mouth derides my enemies, because I rejoice in my victory.	And Mary said, 'My soul magnifies the Lord, and my spirit rejoices in God my Savior,
There is no Holy One like the LORD, no one besides you; there is no Rock like our God.	for the Mighty One has done great things for me, and holy is his name.
The bows of the mighty are broken, but the feeble gird on strength.	He has brought down the powerful from their thrones, and lifted up the lowly;
Those who were full have hired themselves out for bread, but those who were hungry are fat with spoil. The barren has borne seven, but she who has many children is forlorn.'	He has filled the hungry with good things, and sent the rich away empty.'

In addition to being aware of the Jewish identity of these various women, another awareness to bring to our reading of scripture is the unique viewpoint of each evangelist. Below is a compilation of all the texts in the Gospels and Acts that reference Mary. They are grouped by writer chronologically. Those texts which appear in the Sunday lectionary are in normal type face whereas those texts which do not are in bold. Enjoy!

MARY AS PRESENTED BY MARK

Mark 3:31-35

31Then his mother and his brothers came; and standing outside, they sent to him and called him. 32A crowd was sitting around him; and they said to him, "Your mother and your brothers and sisters are outside, asking for you." 33And he replied, "Who are my mother and my brothers?" 34And looking at those who sat around him, he said, "Here are my mother and my brothers! 35Whoever does the will of God is my brother and sister and mother."

Mark 6:1-6

6He left that place and came to his hometown, and his disciples followed him. 2On the sabbath he began to teach in the synagogue, and many who heard him were astounded.

They said, "Where did this man get all this? What is this wisdom that has been given to him? What deeds of power are being done by his hands! ³Is not this the carpenter, the son of Mary and brother of James and Joses and Judas and Simon, and are not his sisters here with us?" And they took offense at him. ⁴Then Jesus said to them, "Prophets are not without honor, except in their hometown, and among their own kin, and in their own house." ⁵And he could do no deed of power there, except that he laid his hands on a few sick people and cured them. ⁶And he was amazed at their unbelief. *(14th Sunday Ordinary Time, Cycle B)*

MARY AS PRESENTED BY MATTHEW

Matthew 1:18-2:23

¹⁸Now the birth of Jesus the Messiah took place in this way. When his mother Mary had been engaged to Joseph, but before they lived together, she was found to be with child from the Holy Spirit. ¹⁹Her husband Joseph, being a righteous man and unwilling to expose her to public disgrace, planned to dismiss her quietly. ²⁰But just when he had resolved to do this, an angel of the Lord appeared to him in a dream and said, "Joseph, son of David, do not be afraid to take Mary as your wife, for the child conceived in her is from the Holy Spirit. ²¹She will bear a son, and you are to name him Jesus, for he will save his people from their sins." ²²All this took place to fulfill what had been spoken by the Lord through the prophet: ²³"Look, the virgin shall conceive and bear a son, and they shall name him Emmanuel," which means, "God is with us." ²⁴When Joseph awoke from sleep, he did as the angel of the Lord commanded him; he took her as his wife, *(Fourth Sunday of Advent, Cycle A)* **²⁵but had no marital relations with her until she had borne a son; and he named him Jesus.**

2In the time of King Herod, after Jesus was born in Bethlehem of Judea, wise men from the East came to Jerusalem, ²asking, "Where is the child who has been born king of the Jews? For we observed his star at its rising, and have come to pay him homage." ³When King Herod heard this, he was frightened, and all Jerusalem with him; ⁴and calling together all the chief priests and scribes of the people, he inquired of them where the Messiah was to be born. ⁵They told him, "In Bethlehem of Judea; for so it has been written by the prophet: ⁶"And you, Bethlehem, in the land of Judah, are by no means least among the rulers of Judah; for from you shall come a ruler who is to shepherd my people Israel.'" ⁷Then Herod secretly called for the wise men and learned from them the exact time when the star had appeared. ⁸Then he sent them to Bethlehem, saying, "Go and search diligently for the child; and when you have found him, bring me word so that

I may also go and pay him homage."

⁹When they had heard the king, they set out; and there, ahead of them, went the star that they had seen at its rising, until it stopped over the place where the child was. ¹⁰When they saw that the star had stopped, they were overwhelmed with joy. ¹¹On entering the house, they saw the child with Mary his mother; and they knelt down and paid him homage. Then, opening their treasure chests, they offered him gifts of gold, frankincense, and myrrh. ¹²And having been warned in a dream not to return to Herod, they left for their own country by another road. *(Epiphany, ABC Cycles)*

¹³Now after they had left, an angel of the Lord appeared to Joseph in a dream and said, "Get up, take the child and his mother, and flee to Egypt, and remain there until I tell you; for Herod is about to search for the child, to destroy him." ¹⁴Then Joseph got up, took the child and his mother by night, and went to Egypt, ¹⁵and remained there until the death of Herod. This was to fulfill what had been spoken by the Lord through the prophet, "Out of Egypt I have called my son."

¹⁶When Herod saw that he had been tricked by the wise men, he was infuriated, and he sent and killed all the children in and around Bethlehem who were two years old or under, according to the time that he had learned from the wise men. ¹⁷Then was fulfilled what had been spoken through the prophet Jeremiah: ¹⁸"A voice was heard in Ramah, wailing and loud lamentation, Rachel weeping for her children; she refused to be consoled, because they are no more."

¹⁹When Herod died, an angel of the Lord suddenly appeared in a dream to Joseph in Egypt and said, ²⁰"Get up, take the child and his mother, and go to the land of Israel, for those who were seeking the child's life are dead." ²¹Then Joseph got up, took the child and his mother, and went to the land of Israel. ²²But when he heard that Archelaus was ruling over Judea in place of his father Herod, he was afraid to go there. And after being warned in a dream, he went away to the district of Galilee. ²³There he made his home in a town called Nazareth, so that what had been spoken through the prophets might be fulfilled, "He will be called a Nazorean." *(Sunday in the Octave of Christmas, Cycle A)*

Matthew 12:46-50

⁴⁶While he was still speaking to the crowds, his mother and his brothers were standing outside, wanting to speak to him. ⁴⁷Someone told him, "Look, your mother and your brothers are standing outside, wanting to speak to you." ⁴⁸But to the one who had told him this, Jesus replied, "Who is my mother, and who are my brothers?" ⁴⁹And pointing to his disciples, he said, "Here are my

mother and my brothers! ⁵⁰For whoever does the will of my Father in heaven is my brother and sister and mother."

MARY AS PRESENTED BY LUKE

Luke 1:26-56

²⁶In the sixth month the angel Gabriel was sent by God to a town in Galilee called Nazareth, ²⁷to a virgin engaged to a man whose name was Joseph, of the house of David. The virgin's name was Mary. ²⁸And he came to her and said, "Greetings, favored one! The Lord is with you." ²⁹But she was much perplexed by his words and pondered what sort of greeting this might be. ³⁰The angel said to her, "Do not be afraid, Mary, for you have found favor with God. ³¹And now, you will conceive in your womb and bear a son, and you will name him Jesus. ³²He will be great, and will be called the Son of the Most High, and the Lord God will give to him the throne of his ancestor David.

³³He will reign over the house of Jacob forever, and of his kingdom there will be no end." ³⁴Mary said to the angel, "How can this be, since I am a virgin?" ³⁵The angel said to her, "The Holy Spirit will come upon you, and the power of the Most High will overshadow you; therefore the child to be born will be holy; he will be called Son of God. ³⁶And now, your relative Elizabeth in her old age has also conceived a son; and this is the sixth month for her who was said to be barren. ³⁷For nothing will be impossible with God." ³⁸Then Mary said, "Here am I, the servant of the Lord; let it be with me according to your word." Then the angel departed from her. (Fourth Sunday of Advent, Cycle B)

³⁹In those days Mary set out and went with haste to a Judean town in the hill country, ⁴⁰where she entered the house of Zechariah and greeted Elizabeth. ⁴¹When Elizabeth heard Mary's greeting, the child leaped in her womb. And Elizabeth was filled with the Holy Spirit ⁴²and exclaimed with a loud cry, "Blessed are you among women, and blessed is the fruit of your womb. ⁴³And why has this happened to me, that the mother of my Lord comes to me? ⁴⁴For as soon as I heard the sound of your greeting, the child in my womb leaped for joy. ⁴⁵And blessed is she who believed that there would be a fulfillment of what was spoken to her by the Lord." *(Fourth Sunday of Advent, Cycle C)* **⁴⁶And Mary said, "My soul magnifies the Lord, ⁴⁷and my spirit rejoices in God my Savior, ⁴⁸for he has looked with favor on the lowliness of his servant. Surely, from now on all generations will call me blessed; ⁴⁹for the Mighty One has done great things for me, and holy is his name. ⁵⁰His mercy is for those who fear him from generation to generation. ⁵¹He has shown strength with his arm; he has scattered the proud in the thoughts of their hearts. ⁵²He has brought**

down the powerful from their thrones, and lifted up the lowly; [53]he has filled the hungry with good things, and sent the rich away empty. [54]He has helped his servant Israel, in remembrance of his mercy, [55]according to the promise he made to our ancestors, to Abraham and to his descendants forever." [56]And Mary remained with her about three months and then returned to her home.

Luke 2:1-56

In those days a decree went out from Emperor Augustus that all the world should be registered. [2]This was the first registration and was taken while Quirinius was governor of Syria. [3]All went to their own towns to be registered. [4]Joseph also went from the town of Nazareth in Galilee to Judea, to the city of David called Bethlehem, because he was descended from the house and family of David. [5]He went to be registered with Mary, to whom he was engaged and who was expecting a child. [6]While they were there, the time came for her to deliver her child. [7]And she gave birth to her firstborn son and wrapped him in bands of cloth, and laid him in a manger, because there was no place for them in the inn.

[8]In that region there were shepherds living in the fields, keeping watch over their flock by night. [9]Then an angel of the Lord stood before them, and the glory of the Lord shone around them, and they were terrified. [10]But the angel said to them, "Do not be afraid; for see—I am bringing you good news of great joy for all the people: [11]to you is born this day in the city of David a Savior, who is the Messiah, the Lord. [12]This will be a sign for you: you will find a child wrapped in bands of cloth and lying in a manger." [13]And suddenly there was with the angel a multitude of the heavenly host, praising God and saying, [14]"Glory to God in the highest heaven, and on earth peace among those whom he favors!" (*Christmas, Midnight Mass, A,B,C Cycles*) [15]When the angels had left them and gone into heaven, the shepherds said to one another, "Let us go now to Bethlehem and see this thing that has taken place, which the Lord has made known to us." [16]So they went with haste and found Mary and Joseph, and the child lying in the manger. [17]When they saw this, they made known what had been told them about this child; [18]and all who heard it were amazed at what the shepherds told them. [19]But Mary treasured all these words and pondered them in her heart. [20](*Christmas, Mass at Dawn, A,B,C*) **The shepherds returned, glorifying and praising God for all they had heard and seen, as it had been told them.** [21]After eight days had passed, it was time to circumcise the child; and he was called Jesus, the name given by the angel before he was conceived in the womb. [22]When the time came for their purification according to the law of Moses, they brought him up to Jerusalem to present him to the Lord [23](as it is written

in the law of the Lord, "Every firstborn male shall be designated as holy to the Lord"), ²⁴and they offered a sacrifice according to what is stated in the law of the Lord, "a pair of turtledoves or two young pigeons."

²⁵Now there was a man in Jerusalem whose name was Simeon; this man was righteous and devout, looking forward to the consolation of Israel, and the Holy Spirit rested on him. ²⁶It had been revealed to him by the Holy Spirit that he would not see death before he had seen the Lord's Messiah. ²⁷Guided by the Spirit, Simeon came into the temple; and when the parents brought in the child Jesus, to do for him what was customary under the law, ²⁸Simeon took him in his arms and praised God, saying, ²⁹"Master, now you are dismissing your servant in peace, according to your word; ³⁰for my eyes have seen your salvation, ³¹which you have prepared in the presence of all peoples, ³²a light for revelation to the Gentiles and for glory to your people Israel." ³³And the child's father and mother were amazed at what was being said about him. ³⁴Then Simeon blessed them and said to his mother Mary, "This child is destined for the falling and the rising of many in Israel, and to be a sign that will be opposed ³⁵so that the inner thoughts of many will be revealed—and a sword will pierce your own soul too." ³⁶There was also a prophet, Anna the daughter of Phanuel, of the tribe of Asher. She was of a great age, having lived with her husband seven years after her marriage, ³⁷then as a widow to the age of eighty-four. She never left the temple but worshiped there with fasting and prayer night and day. ³⁸At that moment she came, and began to praise God and to speak about the child to all who were looking for the redemption of Jerusalem. ³⁹When they had finished everything required by the law of the Lord, they returned to Galilee, to their own town of Nazareth. ⁴⁰The child grew and became strong, filled with wisdom; and the favor of God was upon him. (*Sunday in the Octave of Christmas, Cycle B*)

⁴¹Now every year his parents went to Jerusalem for the festival of the Passover. ⁴²And when he was twelve years old, they went up as usual for the festival. ⁴³When the festival was ended and they started to return, the boy Jesus stayed behind in Jerusalem, but his parents did not know it. ⁴⁴Assuming that he was in the group of travelers, they went a day's journey. Then they started to look for him among their relatives and friends. ⁴⁵When they did not find him, they returned to Jerusalem to search for him. ⁴⁶After three days they found him in the temple, sitting among the teachers, listening to them and asking them questions. ⁴⁷And all who heard him were amazed at his understanding and his answers. ⁴⁸When his parents saw him they were astonished; and his mother said to him, "Child, why have you treated us like this? Look, your father and I have been searching for you in great anxiety." ⁴⁹He said to them, "Why were you searching for me?

Did you not know that I must be in my Father's house?" [50]But they did not understand what he said to them. [51]Then he went down with them and came to Nazareth, and was obedient to them. His mother treasured all these things in her heart. (*Sunday in the Octave of Christmas, Cycle C*)

Luke 4:14-30

[14]Then Jesus, filled with the power of the Spirit, returned to Galilee, and a report about him spread through all the surrounding country. [15]He began to teach in their synagogues and was praised by everyone. [16]When he came to Nazareth, where he had been brought up, he went to the synagogue on the sabbath day, as was his custom. He stood up to read, [17]and the scroll of the prophet Isaiah was given to him. He unrolled the scroll and found the place where it was written: [18]"The Spirit of the Lord is upon me, because he has anointed me to bring good news to the poor. He has sent me to proclaim release to the captives and recovery of sight to the blind, to let the oppressed go free, [19]to proclaim the year of the Lord's favor." [20]And he rolled up the scroll, gave it back to the attendant, and sat down. The eyes of all in the synagogue were fixed on him. [21]Then he began to say to them, "Today this scripture has been fulfilled in your hearing." (*Third Sunday of the Year, Cycle C*) [22]All spoke well of him and were amazed at the gracious words that came from his mouth. They said, "Is not this Joseph's son?" [23]He said to them, 'Doubtless you will quote to me this proverb, 'Doctor, cure yoursel f!' And you will say, 'Do here also in your hometown the things that we have heard you did at Capernaum.'" [24]And he said, "Truly I tell you, no prophet is accepted in the prophet's hometown. [25]But the truth is, there were many widows in Israel in the time of Elijah, when the heaven was shut up three years and six months, and there was a severe famine over all the land; [26]yet Elijah was sent to none of them except to a widow at Zarephath in Sidon. [27]There were also many lepers in Israel in the time of the prophet Elisha, and none of them was cleansed except Naaman the Syrian." [28]When they heard this, all in the synagogue were filled with rage. [29]They got up, drove him out of the town, and led him to the brow of the hill on which their town was built, so that they might hurl him off the cliff. [30]But he passed through the midst of them and went on his way (*Fourth Sunday of the Year, Cycle C*).

Acts 1:12-14

[12]Then they returned to Jerusalem from the mount called Olivet, which is near Jerusalem, a sabbath day's journey away. [13]When they had entered the city, they went to the room upstairs where they were staying, Peter, and John, and James, and Andrew, Philip and Thomas, Bartholomew and Matthew, James son of Alphaeus, and Simon the Zealot, and

Judas son of James. [14]All these were constantly devoting themselves to prayer, together with certain women, including Mary the mother of Jesus, as well as his brothers. (*Seventh Sunday of Easter, Cycle A, preempted in some locations by Pentecost celebrated on a Sunday*).

MARY AS PRESENTED BY JOHN

John 2:1-12

On the third day there was a wedding in Cana of Galilee, and the mother of Jesus was there. [2]Jesus and his disciples had also been invited to the wedding. [3]When the wine gave out, the mother of Jesus said to him, "They have no wine." [4]And Jesus said to her, "Woman, what concern is that to you and to me? My hour has not yet come." [5]His mother said to the servants, "Do whatever he tells you." [6]Now standing there were six stone water jars for the Jewish rites of purification, each holding twenty or thirty gallons. [7]Jesus said to them, "Fill the jars with water." And they filled them up to the brim. [8]He said to them, "Now draw some out, and take it to the chief steward." So they took it. [9]When the steward tasted the water that had become wine, and did not know where it came from (though the servants who had drawn the water knew), the steward called the bridegroom [10]and said to him, "Everyone serves the good wine first, and then the inferior wine after the guests have become drunk. But you have kept the good wine until now." [11]Jesus did this, the first of his signs, in Cana of Galilee, and revealed his glory; and his disciples believed in him. [12]After this he went down to Capernaum with his mother, his brothers, and his disciples; and they remained there a few days. (*Second Sunday of the Year, Cycle C*)

John 19:25-27

[25]And that is what the soldiers did. Meanwhile, standing near the cross of Jesus were his mother, and his mother's sister, Mary the wife of Clopas, and Mary Magdalene. [26]When Jesus saw his mother and the disciple whom he loved standing beside her, he said to his mother, "Woman, here is your son." [27]Then he said to the disciple, "Here is your mother." And from that hour the disciple took her into his own home.

MARY'S PRAYER

NOTE FROM KATHLEEN: *It seems presumptuous to me to offer a prayer that remarks upon Mary's own prayer in the Magnificat. At the same time, the nature of Mary's liberating words calls us to reflect upon and make her words our own. For our prayer this week, I suggest we each create our own Magnificat. To do this, here is a "T-exercise" that allows the words to sink in ever deeper in our hearts.*

STEP ONE: *Choose a particular line of scripture, in this case a line of the Magnificat or one of the other lines from the "omitted scriptures." Write it across the top of the "T" (see example attached).*

STEP TWO: *Along the left hand side of the page paraphrase or write the same words in 21st Century, North Americam, female, 40-something (or whatever) language (see example).*

STEP ONE: *Along the right hand side of the page respond prayerfully to what you have read, written, and felt in language directed toward God (see example).*

For he has looked upon his servant in her lowliness; all ages to come shall call me blessed.

For God has noticed me, ordinary wife, mother and grandmother that I am, seem me as one who seeks to be a faithful follower, and has been pleased. It is in exactly that role that I will be blessed by God and remembered by my family and all whom I love even into the generations to come.	*Dear God, it is humbling to think that you come to me as you came to Mary. You do not find my life too mundane to be a part of your plan. By your grace, and in spite of my flaws, you will bless my family and all those I love—not only by the love that I show but also in the way you redeem my failings and make them work to good as well. What could be more loving than that? Thank you, my God.*

NEVER ON SUNDAY
A Look at the Women NOT in the Lectionary

WEEK SEVEN - MARY

Samuel 1:1-2:11, Mark 3:31-35, 6:1-6, Matthew 1:18-2:23, 12:46-50, Luke 1:26-56, 4:14-30, Acts 1:11-14, John 2:1-12, 19L25-27 (see NT selections in Background: Mary)

1) *Compare Hannah's song or canticle to Mary's. Were you previously aware of the two and how similar they are? What do you think is the basic message of each one about the circumstances, the woman singing and the child born of the woman? What conclusions do you draw from comparing the two songs?*

2) *The scripture selections on Mary are divided by author in "Background: Mary." Read each one and consider the picture it presents of Mary. What would your impression of Mary be if you'd only ever read Mark? Matthew? Luke? John? Which evangelist's image is closest to the one that you hold in your own heart and imagination? Which one is the most different from your own? What surprised you about the comparison?*

3) *The scripture selections on Mary are further marked to show which passages are in the lectionary and which are not. The normal font verses are IN the lectionary (reference is italicized), the bold faced verses are NOT in the lectionary. What did you notice? What surprised you?*

4) *Look at just the selections that are NOT in the lectionary:*

   - *a single line in Matthew, Mt1:25,*
   - *Jesus is confronted by his relatives - Mk 3:31-35 and Mt 12:46-50,*

- *Mary's Magnificat – Lk 1:26-56,*
- *the slaying of the children of Bethlehem – Mt1:18-2:23, and*
- *Mary at the foot of the cross – Jn 19:25-27.*

Which ones would you consider most worthy of including? Why might you choose not to include them? Why?

5) *Choose one of the omitted passages to focus on. Why is it important to you? What message or image does it convey about Mary that makes a difference?*

6) *Using the passage you have chosen, write a Midrash on that passage.*

CHALLENGE

Participate in the "T-exercise" that is suggested for this week's "Mary's Prayer." Come prepared to share your prayer and what it was like for you to create it.

A CLOSER LOOK AT THE TEXT:
MARY

I. MARK 3:31-35, MATTHEW 1:25, MATTHEW 12:46-50

Two of these passages tell the story of Jesus' relatives appearing on the scene of his public ministry while the single line from Mt 1 testifies to the virginal conception of Mary. All three of these passages share the characteristic of being problematic as regards the familial relationship of Mary to Jesus and to Joseph. The problem is in the interpretation of the lines. What does "brothers" or "relatives" mean? What does "until" imply? We can offer evidence and refutation either way. One interpretation explains and preserves the perpetual virginity of Mary (i.e. "brothers" can be broadly, legitimately interpreted to mean extended family, relatives or cousins and "until" does not say anything about after). Another interpretation of the words argues against that (i.e. the text can or "should" be taken to mean what it appears to say unless counter-indicated elsewhere). The case cannot be proved or disproved on the basis of scripture alone.

Ultimately, in the Catholic tradition, the Church has taught and maintained over the length of the centuries that Mary was a virgin at the conception of Jesus and remained a virgin throughout her life. The weight of Church authority, of itself, however is not a compelling argument for those who do not share a Roman Catholic affiliation. And even among Catholics who may accept the teaching, the importance or centrality of that teaching may carry varying weight.

For our purposes it is enough to recognize the potential within these lines for emotional argumentation and acknowledge that this may be the reason they do not appear in the Sunday lectionary.

II. MATTHEW 2:16-18

These three lines contain such blood-chilling violence that it is not surprising they are neatly excised from the Christmas story and season. Yet it is historical fact that the Son of God was born into a period of extreme political chaos. History records that Herod killed two brother-in-laws, his own wife Marianme, and two of his own sons. In anticipation of his own death, he ordered the round-up and arrest of 200 ordinary citizens that he decreed be executed on the day he died—all to ensure there be a proper atmosphere of mourning for his funeral. The slaying of children in Bethlehem would be but a minor footnote to the multiple atrocities Herod committed.

Yet what lessons does this episode hold for us?

The Son of God chose not only the lowliness of the stable; he also was exposed to the same kind of grave danger as those living under one of the most infamous of despots. From the flight into Egypt to standing before the ruthless and notorious Pontius Pilate, Jesus suffered at the hands of the cruel and powerful. At every juncture, his life was lived in solidarity with those most dispossessed and powerless. All humanity is caught in the clutches of whatever time and place we occupy and Jesus was no exception.

While Joseph is the main character in Matthew's infancy narrative—he is the one who experiences dreams and makes decisions, we cannot help but wonder at Mary's reaction and his.

Did they even guess at the tragedy awaiting their neighbors? If not, when did they get word? What grief, relief and regret did that engender? Does not the saving hand of God always raise questions about those tragedies not averted? Matthew's gospel, especially in these few lines, is full of troubling, mysterious questions. The miracle of the Incarnation embraces these questions as surely as it glows warmly from a nativity scene.

III. JOHN 19:25-27

Each evangelist has subtle variations at the cross scene. Not surprisingly Mark and Matthew are the most similar: "There were also women looking on from a distance; among them were Mary Magdalene, and Mary the mother of James the younger and of Joses, and Salome. These used to follow him and provided for him when he was in Galilee; and there were many other women who had come up with him to Jerusalem" (Mk 15:40-41). "Many women were also there, looking on from a distance; they had followed Jesus from Galilee and had provided for him. [56]Among them were Mary Magdalene, and Mary the mother of James and Joseph, and the mother of the sons of Zebedee" (Mt. 27:55-56).

Luke is less specific, "all his acquaintances, including the women who had followed him from Galilee, stood at a distance, watching these things" (Lk 23:39).

John changes only slightly the names of the women: Mary Magdalene is repeated, Mary the wife of Clopas is included is the sister of Mary his mother and Mary herself is included. But he makes a significant shift in location. Whereas the other evangelists all use the phrase "from (or at) a distance," John says, "standing near the cross of Jesus." He also includes "the disciple whom he loved" standing beside Mary. Only in that proximity could such an intimate conversation take place.

IV. LUKE 1:46-55
Magnificat as poetry/song

Luke has four hymns or canticles in his gospel: Mary's Magnificat, Zechariah's Canticles (1:67-79), the angel's Gloria (2:13-14) and Simeon's Canticle (2:28-32). In all four, the structure and the theme are patterned on the hymns of praise that would be part of Jewish prayer at the time of Jesus. They exultantly praise and thank God and use images that recall God's saving action in Jewish history even as they celebrate God's present saving action in a life transforming way. They look to the past but also anticipate a future of triumphant hope.

The Magnificat can be divided into four unified stanzas: (a) introductory praise of God (1:46b-47), (b) lines that highlight God's saving action toward Mary (1:48-50), (c) lines that emphasize God's saving deeds toward Israel (1:51-53), (c) testimony to covenant mercy and faithfulness (1:54-55).

(a) The opening lines show a characteristic of Hebrew poetry that is often evidenced in the psalms, synonymous parallels. Here phrases mirror one another—"my soul" mirrors "my spirit" and "proclaims the greatness" mirrors "has found gladness.' This creates a balance that reinforces the theme even as it amplifies it. Thus, the soul or spirit of Mary both declares the greatness of God and finds delight in God.

(b) The reasons for such joy are given in these next set of lines. In the Greek, both verses 48 and 49 begin with hoti, meaning "because/for"—again a parallel structure: "because he has looked with favor on the lowliness of his servant;" and "because the Mighty One has done great things for me."

(c) In this third set of lines we have a triad of contrasting parallels: the proud are reversed by those of low estate, the mighty by the lowly, and the rich by the hungry.

Thus we have reversals of the moral, social and economic dimensions. In the Greek all six verbs are in a tense unique to Greek, the aorist tense. This holds both the future and the present, meaning it refers to a future but it also brings about the future in the present. The effect of the action of the verb has already been achieved. Thus the reversals referred to not only will happen but in the present moment to which they refer, they have, happened.

(d) These closing lines of praise recall God's covenant with "his servant Israel" and celebrate the ultimate fulfillment of God's promised faithfulness and mercy.

Magnificat as journey

The scope of the Magnificat sweeps through the whole of Judeo-Christian biblical theology from Abraham and Sarah through Mary to the future through the end of time. Revolutionary in language and concept, it praises the God who is faithful and has been faithful, dwelling with all those who suffer. It passionately calls believers into that same saving action, to be one with all oppressed peoples so as to participate in the liberation that God both promises and brings about.

In her words Mary lifts up the immediate moment, the small horizon, to the grand vision of God's breaking in upon humanity. Thus her words echo her physical reality. As the natural mother, she gives birth and nurses life biologically; as a disciple of Jesus (a Lukan theme), she bears Christ to the world and nurtures that life to fulfillment. This pre-figures the later lines of Luke, "Blessed is the womb that bore you and the breasts that nursed you!" (Lk. 11:27).

The *Catechism of the Catholic Church*, thus, sees Mary's prayer as the prayer of the Church:

> That is why the Canticle of Mary, the Magnificat (Latin) or Megalynei (Byzantine) is the song both of the Mother of God and of the Church; the song of the Daughter of Zion and of the new People of God; the song of thanksgiving for the fullness of graces poured out in the economy of salvation and the song of the "poor" whose hope is met by the fulfillment of the promises made to our ancestors, "to Abraham and to his posterity for ever." (#2619)

MEANWHILE, ON SUNDAY MORNING....

The texts listed as not appearing on Sunday are all assigned to other weekday or holy day readings. Mark's story of Jesus' relatives appears on Tuesday of the Third Week of the Year whereas Matthew's story of the relatives appears on Tuesday of the Sixteenth Week of the Year. Mt 2:16-19, Herod's slaying of the children of Bethlehem is assigned to December 28th, the Feast of the Holy Innocents. Mary's Magnificat is read on both the Feast of the Visitation, May 31st, and the Feast of the Assumption, August 15, the only one of all these dates listed to be a holy day of obligation. John's story of Mary at the foot of the cross is the gospel reading for the Feast of Our Lady of Sorrow, September 15th. Additionally, the Magnificat is part of the Liturgy of the Hours and, so, is prayed or sung at Morning Prayer daily.

THE
BENT
WOMAN
IN
LUKE

BACKGROUND:
THE BENT WOMAN IN LUKE

As we enter into the "familiar" territory of the Gospels, the challenge shifts from learning something new to re-learning, finding something previously unseen, in that which we think we already know. We need to move beyond the received, assumed meaning(s) that we bring with us when we approach a text. An important consideration is to look at the authors of each of the four gospels—Matthew, Mark, Luke and John, and some of the unique characteristics of each of these four familiar writers.

Matthew, Mark and Luke are referred to as the *synoptic* gospels which means, literally "seen with one eye." They parallel one another and have much in common. Mark was the first gospel written, about 65 AD. Both Matthew and Luke draw from Mark and from another common, outside, but undiscovered, source that scripture scholars call "Q"or "quelle" which is German for the word "source." Both Matthew and Luke wrote about 85 AD. Each wrote to a different audience for a specific purpose which helped determine the choices made in what to include and how to say it. John shares much less with the other three and has a large amount of material unique to that Gospel. It is written significantly later, about 100 AD, and is markedly different in style as well as purpose.

MARK

The earliest of the gospels, Mark was drawn from by both Matthew and Luke in the writing of their gospels. The time frame for Mark corresponds to about one generation from the passion-death-and-resurrection event of Jesus. The earliest followers of Jesus had no scriptures. When they gathered in worship they used the Hebrew scriptures and, later, shared the letters that Paul sent to them. They told the stories as received first-hand. It was not until the first generation was dying off and the expected parousia, or second-coming of Jesus, did not appear imminent in that generation, that the need existed for writing down the stories. Scholars differ in their opinion on the location for Mark's composition but the intended audience was Greek-speaking and largely literate. Most early Christians, however, were from the middle and lower classes and, therefore, illiterate. The Gospel of Mark was meant, then, to be read aloud and is written for the ear rather than the eye. As such, repetition, summaries, prologues, epilogues, key words, foreshadowing, plot synopses, etc. provided listening helps from within the text and assisted the ancient listener even as they may baffle the modern reader.

One of Mark's literary devices to assist the listener is to lay out the plot simply, rather like a play. In this play, the identity of Jesus is the key mystery. It is revealed to the listener early on, at the very outset, in fact, at the Baptism by John when the Voice says, "You are my Son, the Beloved" (Mk 1:11). It is echoed at the end of Mark's gospel in the words of the centurion at the foot of the cross, "Truly this man was God's son" (Mk 15:39). In the middle however there is much question about Jesus' identity and those most caught up in the confusion are the apostles who never seem to get it right, even as various demons repeatedly recognize Jesus for who he is. Against the blatant inability of the Twelve to recognize Jesus or his message and their failure of him in his hour of greatest need, the women come off quite well though not well developed. They are the only faithful group of followers to be found at either the cross or the tomb. With the exception of Herodias, they are all positive figures who respond to his message or are healed by him.

MATTHEW

Matthew writes to an early Christian group that was largely Jewish but that has begun to incorporate some Gentiles. Throughout the gospel, Matthew emphasizes Jewish concerns and points out how Jesus fulfills various prophecies from the scriptures. Another characteristic of Matthew is that of teaching. Amid miracles, healings and stories of controversy, five major teaching discourses are laid out within the ministry of Jesus: the Sermon on the Mount (chapters 5-7), missionary teachings (chapter 10), parables on the Kingdom of God (chapter 13), instructions to and about the church (chapter 18), and predictions on the end time (chapters 24-25).

In addition to being a teacher, Matthew is a political activist. He consistently highlights those persons removed from the source of religious and political power. His emphasis on service frequently extols women and they often appear apart from their household, husband, father or son and take on active roles.

The two opening chapters, the genealogy and birth of Christ are unique to Matthew. The genealogy shows Matthew's concern for Jesus as the predicted Messiah and the fulfillment of the Mosaic Law. His infancy material begins with setting a Mosaic scene where once again, an evil king orders the death of Hebrew babies and one special child is saved. Matthew tells the story through the experience of Joseph and by his example of obedience the role of father is defined as one who serves rather than rules over.

LUKE

The Gospel of Luke is the first part of a two-part writing for the Acts of the Apostles continues the story begun in Luke. A gifted story-teller, Luke creates a text that is, perhaps, the most readable of the four gospels. The author was probably a Gentile Christian, well educated in Hellenistic literature and thought and familiar enough with the Greek translation of the Hebrew Bible to imitate its style, blend sources, and be theologically creative.

Luke is known as the "Gospel of the poor," a fitting title. Luke's concern for the marginalized and the poor is consistent and apparent throughout the gospel. This gospel is also sometimes called the "Gospel of women" because it contains so much unique material that centers on women. Despite that reputation, however, the Gospel of Luke is problematic for women. Written at a time when Christians were beginning to be suspected and persecuted, Luke goes out of his way to portray women as prayerful, quiet, grateful, supportive of men, and foregoing leadership. He is very concerned to show that this new religion and its founder were not revolutionary and therefore were not dangerous to the state. Judaism had enjoyed protection under Roman law and that protection was eroding as the two traditions drifted away from one another. Thus, Luke has a vested interest in presenting law-abiding women and men. His portrayal of women may have also been a "corrective" to the roles of leadership that women had taken on in early Christian household churches, a possible source of scandal or criticism.

JOHN

All four of the New Testament Gospels are distinct portraits of the life, ministry, death and resurrection of Jesus. They all four share some key stories like the feeding of the five thousand and Jesus' walking on water as well as lengthy accounts of Jesus' passion and death. There are other ways, however, in which John's Gospel is significantly different from the synoptics. Mark, Matthew and Luke, for example, all have Jesus begin his ministry in Galilee and move into Judea only once where his journey to Jerusalem ends with his crucifixion. John, however, has Jesus' ministry alternate between Galilee and Jerusalem to which he makes three different trips. The synoptics narrate a ministry of about one year whereas John spans a three year period for Jesus' ministry. The parables that one finds so common in the synoptics are rarely seen in John. The style is vastly different as well. Both Mark and John ask the question, who is Jesus? Mark sets out to answer that question in dramatic, stylized form. John invites the reader into the question offering multiple titles for Jesus, figurative language, extensive dialogue and mystical language as in Jesus' own "I am" statements.

The opening is an immediate clue to the nature of this gospel as it opens, not with story, but with a song referred to as the Prologue to John, "In the beginning was the Word..." (Jn 1:1). Hearkening back to Genesis itself, the scope of John is deliberately large.

Women play significant roles in the Gospel of John. This is evidenced not only by the number of stories that include women but also by the theological significance of the stories. They are the main conversation partners with Jesus in three stories that reveal his identity, his mission, and the nature of discipleship, (Jn. 4:14-42 - the Samaritan woman at the well, Jn. 7:53-8:11 - the woman caught in adultery, Jn. 11:1-44 – Martha after the death of Lazarus).

PRAYER OF THE
BENT WOMAN

When Jesus saw her, he called her over and said, 'Woman, you are set free from your ailment.' When he laid his hands on her, immediately she stood up straight and began praising God (Luke 13:12-13).

Call out to us, O God of all women bent over. We are your daughters but we have forgotten.

Too long we've been weary, burdened, depressed.

We've believed our pain was of our own making and seen no future beyond the same.

We no longer know to ask for healing, for something better.

But you, Son of Mary, you have not forgotten;

you take notice of those whom no one else sees.

Make straight the twisted logic that blames our own souls. Call us to yourself, touch our brokenness, restore well-being, recall our dignity, so that...

free to stand tall,

we may glance upward to search your face, and in your eyes, see a beloved daughter of God.

Amen.

- KMcK

NEVER ON SUNDAY
A Look at the Women NOT in the Lectionary

WEEK EIGHT - THE BENT WOMAN IN LUKE

Luke 13:10-17

1) *Are you personally familiar with this story? If so, from where? Check in with the other women in your group to gauge their familiarity.*

2) *The woman is introduced as having been possessed by a spirit for 18 years, a spirit which had drained her strength. Irregular medical conditions were attributed in this era to possession by evil spirits. What might this woman's own understanding of her affliction be after 18 years? Her self esteem?*

3) *The gospel says, "she was bent over and was quite unable to stand up straight" (Lk 13:11). What kind of world view would this woman have after facing the ground for 18 years?*

4) *Did she ask for healing? Who initiated the interaction? Was there any testimony of faith required? Can you think of another biblical incident where Jesus is the one who initiates a healing? Why do you think Jesus did what he did? What does this say about the heart of Jesus?*

5) *Jesus addresses the chief of the synagogue and cites his letting out an ox or ass from its stall on the Sabbath and then asks rhetorically if this "daughter of Abraham" should not be similarly be freed from her shackles on the Sabbath. How does the image of fettered animal compare to this woman before her encounter with Jesus? How does it compare to her being hailed as a "daughter of Abraham?" How might that have sounded to her after suffering her affliction for so long?*

6) *In straightening her back, the woman's spirit is also cured. Which, in your opinion, is the greater healing?*

7) *Jesus encounters this woman in the synagogue. The indignation expressed at his healing her is not directed toward her being there so we may surmise that a woman's presence was not exceptional. This tells us something about women and worship at this time but it also underscores her invisibility. Why did Jesus notice her? What might we conclude from his attention to her?*

8) *Write a Midrash as this woman, a relative of hers, an onlooker, etc.*

CHALLENGE

Consider who you know in your circle of friends, work, neighborhood, parish, etc. who might, like the Bent Woman, suffer from an accumulated lack of regard and respect to the point of being inwardly weighed down, bent over. How might you restore her dignity, treat her as a "Daughter of Abraham?" Begin with the Prayer of the Bent Woman and decide on an actions step of kindness and respect.

A CLOSER LOOK AT THE TEXT:
THE BENT WOMAN IN LUKE

In last week's lesson Mary proclaimed that God would "lift up the lowly" (Lk 1:52). This week her son does exactly that in this story from Luke. He lifts up this woman physically in straightening her bent back and allowing her face to see and be seen. He lifts her up socially in calling her out of anonymity into the heart of the synagogue community. He lifts her up spiritually by breaking the bonds of Satan and restoring her dignity as a daughter of Abraham.

She represents all those for whom Jesus has come to establish God's Kingdom. She is unnamed, as are most of the people in the world. Her bent back could be a physical disease such as osteoporosis—such diseases were thought to be due to sinfulness, or she could be bent by years of hard labor like the millions who labor in fields or rice paddies, porter loads or haul water. She is expendable and unnoticed—as are most people.

In using the phrase, "daughter of Abraham," Jesus recalls her connection to the long line that went before her. Her ancestors were freed by Yahweh from slavery in Egypt. Twice in Israel's history an eighteen year period has had special significance. After eighteen years the Israelites were freed from Moabite oppression in Judges 3:1-4. They were rescued from the Ammonites after eighteen years in Judges 10:1-18. As a daughter of Abraham she shares in that saving history. She, too, is in bondage but she, too, inherits God promise of faithfulness. She represents all those who have gone before and hoped in God's deliverance. She is anyone who is not free, who cannot stand tall, who has no voice for singing or praising but who responds with immediate praise to the presence of Christ. Her greatest gift may well be that the first sight her lifting face alights upon is the face of Jesus.

This story of the bent woman is an example of a pericope. A pericope (pe-RIH-co-pee) refers to a literary unit, a selection or extract taken from a book. It is a term used by biblical scholars to refer to a portion of scripture that stands on its own. Frequently there are headings in the Bible that are meant to define such pericopes. In studying the bent woman in Luke, it might be argued that the pericope should be extended to include the two short parables that follow. While the subject seems to shift from the woman, the setting does not change and Jesus' words are clearly a continuation, "Then he said..." (Lk 13:18). Looked at this way, the two parables would tell us something about the bent woman as well. Her healing is still the subject of the parables and she becomes, like the mustard seed and the yeast, a sign of the Kingdom of God

In the setting of the synagogue, Jesus cured the woman and shamed his opponents but caused the people to rejoice. He speaks then to these same people, inviting them to become a community modeled on the kingdom, a place that provides shelter for growth.

The mustard plant is a bush more than a tree and hardy, growing wildly, even along dirt roads. Its density invites flocks of birds who forage through its branches and call back and forth. While not always welcomed by gardeners and farmers, it certainly attracts birds. A community that shelters a seed of hope, that offers hospitality to those without home, respect, value or significance—that is the Kingdom of God.

In the second parable the Kingdom of God is compared to the yeast a woman takes and adds to three measures of flour until all of it is leavened. Those of you who have kneaded bread know what it is to work the dough, to stretch, roll, fold, and shape it and then allow it to expand and take on the shape you have given it. Like the birds hidden in the branches, the yeast hidden in the dough does its work. Again the result is a community that becomes the Kingdom of God. Megan McKenna describes it:

> Jesus singled out a women hidden in the synagogue community and lifted her up, liberating and freeing her to praise God. She is yeast in the community, now active and churning through the whole group. Jesus has been kneading dough and making bread by his healings and touch, his hands-on lifting up. Now the kingdom and the church will be the place where these hidden people of society can impact others. In fact those once thought to be "unclean" and certainly undesirable are now the ones who will permeate the whole group and cause it to grow past its borders and boundaries. This is the experience of Luke's community as described in Acts. (Megan McKenna, Leave Her Alone, p. 61, Orbis Books, Maryknoll, NY, 2000).

Like so many incidents in the Gospels, the conflict that Jesus has with authorities centers around the Sabbath. In Mark, Jesus states it succinctly, "The Sabbath was made for humankind, and not humankind for the Sabbath" (Mk 2:6). In preferring this woman to the Sabbath, Jesus is also saying that no law, no matter how good or holy, should be used to oppress human beings, for people are greater than any law.

Many of the stories of the Gospels have to do with a healing followed by a conflict. This story of the Bent Woman could be seen as just another one of those. Or it could be seen as a story that gives voice, visibility, dignity and hope to those most disenfranchised, especially for those who are women.

MEANWHILE, ON SUNDAY MORNING....

Despite Jesus' calling this woman from obscurity into the light of grace, she disappears again in terms of the lectionary. This pericope was not included in the Lukan, "C," cycle. It is only read on Monday in the Thirtieth Week of Ordinary Time.

THE WOMEN WHO FOLLOWED JESUS

BACKGROUND:
THE WOMEN WHO FOLLOWED JESUS

The synoptics have Jesus' ministry progress as a single journey from Galilee to Jerusalem. Women who follow Jesus on that journey are referred to as a discernable group only in Luke. And only Luke names some of the women in the course of the journey. He takes the list of women mentioned in Mark 15:40 and adds his own and notations:

> Soon afterwards he went on through cities and villages, proclaiming and bringing the good news of the kingdom of God. The twelve were with him, as well as some women who had been cured of evil spirits and infirmities: Mary, called Magdalene, from whom seven demons had gone out, and Joanna, the wife of Herod's steward Chuza, and Susanna, and many others, who provided for them out of their resources (Luke 8:1-3).

All four gospels place women at the scene of the crucifixion. Here are the lines from each that attest to their presence:

Mark 15:40-41,47

40There were also women looking on from a distance; among them were Mary Magdalene, and Mary the mother of James the younger and of Joses, and Salome. 41These used to follow him and provided for him when he was in Galilee; and there were many other women who had come up with him to Jerusalem. 47Mary Magdalene and Mary the mother of Joses saw where the body was laid. *(Passion Sunday, Cycle B, long form—the short form omits these passages and ends just before them).*

Matthew 27:55-61

[55]Many women were also there, looking on from a distance; they had followed Jesus from Galilee and had provided for him. [56]Among them were Mary Magdalene, and Mary the mother of James and Joseph, and the mother of the sons of Zebedee.

[57]When it was evening, there came a rich man from Arimathea, named Joseph, who was also a disciple of Jesus. [58]He went to Pilate and asked for the body of Jesus; then Pilate ordered it to be given to him. [59]So Joseph took the body and wrapped it in a clean linen cloth [60]and laid it in his own new tomb, which he had hewn in the rock. He then rolled a great stone to the door of the tomb and went away. [61]Mary Magdalene and the other Mary were there, sitting opposite the tomb. *(Passion Sunday, Cycle A, long form—the short form omits these passages and ends just before them).*

Luke 23:49-56

[49]But all his acquaintances, including the women who had followed him from Galilee, stood at a distance, watching these things.

[50]Now there was a good and righteous man named Joseph, who, though a member of the council, [51]had not agreed to their plan and action. He came from the Jewish town of Arimathea, and he was waiting expectantly for the kingdom of God. [52]This man went to Pilate and asked for the body of Jesus. [53]Then he took it down, wrapped it in a linen cloth, and laid it in a rock-hewn tomb where no one had ever been laid. [54]It was the day of Preparation, and the sabbath was beginning. [55]The women who had come with him from Galilee followed, and they saw the tomb and how his body was laid. [56]Then they returned, and prepared spices and ointments.

On the sabbath they rested according to the commandment. *(Passion Sunday, Cycle C, long form—the short form omits these passages and ends just before them).*

John 19:25-27

[25]And that is what the soldiers did. Meanwhile, standing near the cross of Jesus were his mother, and his mother's sister, Mary the wife of Clopas, and Mary Magdalene. [26]When Jesus saw his mother and the disciple whom he loved standing beside her, he said to his mother, "Woman, here is your son." [27]Then he said to the disciple, "Here is your mother." And from that hour the disciple took her into his own home.

All four gospels place women at the tomb as witness to the Resurrection. Here are the lines from each evangelist about that:

Mark 16:1-6

16When the sabbath was over, Mary Magdalene, and Mary the mother of James, and Salome bought spices, so that they might go and anoint him. ²And very early on the first day of the week, when the sun had risen, they went to the tomb. ³They had been saying to one another, "Who will roll away the stone for us from the entrance to the tomb?" ⁴When they looked up, they saw that the stone, which was very large, had already been rolled back. ⁵As they entered the tomb, they saw a young man, dressed in a white robe, sitting on the right side; and they were alarmed. ⁶But he said to them, "Do not be alarmed; you are looking for Jesus of Nazareth, who was crucified. He has been raised; he is not here. Look, there is the place they laid him. *(Easter Vigil, Cycle B)*

Matthew 28:1-10

28After the sabbath, as the first day of the week was dawning, Mary Magdalene and the other Mary went to see the tomb. ²And suddenly there was a great earthquake; for an angel of the Lord, descending from heaven, came and rolled back the stone and sat on it. ³His appearance was like lightning, and his clothing white as snow. ⁴For fear of him the guards shook and became like dead men. ⁵But the angel said to the women, "Do not be afraid; I know that you are looking for Jesus who was crucified. ⁶He is not here; for he has been raised, as he said. Come, see the place where he lay. ⁷Then go quickly and tell his disciples, 'He has been raised from the dead, and indeed he is going ahead of you to Galilee; there you will see him.' This is my message for you." ⁸So they left the tomb quickly with fear and great joy, and ran to tell his disciples. ⁹Suddenly Jesus met them and said, "Greetings!" And they came to him, took hold of his feet, and worshiped him. 10Then Jesus said to them, "Do not be afraid; go and tell my brothers to go to Galilee; there they will see me." *(Easter Vigil, Cycle A)*

Luke 24:1-12

But on the first day of the week, at early dawn, they came to the tomb, taking the spices that they had prepared. ²They found the stone rolled away from the tomb, ³but when they went in, they did not find the body. ⁴While they were perplexed about this, suddenly two men in dazzling clothes stood beside them. ⁵The women were terrified and bowed their faces to the ground, but the men said to them, "Why do you look for the living among the dead? He is not here, but has risen. ⁶Remember how he told you, while he was still in Galilee, [7]that the Son of Man must be handed over to sinners, and be crucified, and on the third day rise again." [8]Then they remembered his words, [9]and returning from the tomb, they told all this to the eleven and to all the rest. [10]Now it was Mary Magdalene, Joanna, Mary the mother of James, and the other women with them who told this to the apostles. [11]But these words seemed to them an idle tale, and they did not believe them. [12]But Peter got up and ran to the tomb; stooping and looking in, he saw the linen cloths by themselves; then he went home, amazed at what had happened. *(Easter Vigil, Cycle C)*

John 20:1-3, 10-18

Early on the first day of the week, while it was still dark, Mary Magdalene came to the tomb and saw that the stone had been removed from the tomb. [2]So she ran and went to Simon Peter and the other disciple, the one whom Jesus loved, and said to them, "They have taken the Lord out of the tomb, and we do not know where they have laid him." [3]Then Peter and the other disciple set out and went toward the tomb. *(Easter Sunday, Cycles A,B,C)*. [10]Then the disciples returned to their homes. [11]But Mary stood weeping outside the tomb. As she wept, she bent over to look into the tomb; [12]and she saw two angels in white, sitting where the body of Jesus had been lying, one at the head and the other at the feet. [13]They said to her, "Woman, why are you weeping?" She said to them, "They have taken away my Lord, and I do not know where they have laid him." [14]When she had said this, she turned around and saw Jesus standing there, but she did not know that it was Jesus. [15]Jesus said to her, "Woman, why are you weeping? Whom are you looking for" Supposing him to be the gardener, she said to him, "Sir, if you have carried him away, tell me where you have laid him, and I will take him away." [16]Jesus said to her, "Mary!" She turned and said to him in Hebrew, "Rabbouni!" (which means Teacher). [17]Jesus said to her, "Do not hold on to me, because I have not yet ascended to the Father. But go to my brothers and say to them, 'I am ascending to my Father and your Father, to my God and your God.'" [18]Mary Magdalene went and announced to the disciples, "I have seen the Lord"; and she told them that he had said these things to her.

All four gospels, place women at both scenes but they offer different names and numbers. An inclusive list of names would be: 1) Mary Magdalene, 2) Mary the mother of James and Joses, 3) Salome (Matthew's gospel lists "the mother of the sons of Zebedee" at the same point and may mean that the two are synonymous), 4) Joanna, 5) the mother of Jesus, 6) the sister of the mother of Jesus, 7) Mary the wife of Clopas, and "those who had followed him from Galilee" (Lk. 23:49). Presumably, "those who had followed him from Galilee could be those listed in Luke 8:1-3 and, again, named in Luke 23:49. Only 8) Susanna is not named the second time.

The significance of these women being present in the life and ministry of Jesus and, most especially, at the death and resurrection is two-fold: 1) their inclusion at all attests to their importance given the *androcentric* nature of the text and 2) it was the testimony of women that provided the basis of the most important traditions of the Christ story—the death, burial and resurrection of Jesus.

To say that the Bible is an androcentric text is to say that it is male-centered in its subject matter, authorship, and perspective. The lives of women tend to be ignored or presented only as they relate to the men in the story. This is not an intentional bias; it simply is. Nor is it specific to the sacred scriptures; this is typical of any writing from antiquity, whether as old as portions of the Hebrew Scriptures or as recent as the Christian Scriptures. The frequency with which women appear in the story of Jesus is striking when compared to the rest of scripture—a fact that may be wasted upon us since we rarely place these stories within their larger context. In the whole of the Hebrew Scriptures a total of 1,426 names are mentioned of which 1,315 are men and only 111 are women. In the Gospels we have the 12 apostles named, with some variations on the names, but we also have this listing of eight specific women along with the notation of "many others." Add to these actual followers of Jesus the number of women who appear in the stories: Martha and Mary, the woman of Samaria, the woman with a hemorrhage, the widow of Naim, the woman caught in adultery, Peter's mother-in-law, the Canaanite woman, Jaures's daughter, the woman who anointed Jesus, the daughters of Jerusalem, Pilate's wife, the bride at Cana, the widow who gave her mite, the servant girl in the courtyard, Herodias, and the women of the infancy narratives, Elizabeth, and Anna.

The basic *kerygma* of Christianity is proclaimed at every Mass: Christ has died, Christ is risen, Christ will come again! This core truth is only available to us because of the faithful witness of the women who were there. Without their presence and without their proclamation of what they witnessed, the Jesus event would consist only of his teachings and miracles; the central event of his life among us would have been lost.

There is no doubt that there existed an unusual social equality in the company of Jesus and in his example and message. He consistently liberated and invited the marginalized which, necessarily, in his culture would include women. There is no hint of his demeaning women, having a double standard or in any way relegating them to lesser worth. In Jesus we encounter a man who is fully integrated, willing and able to accept women as partners in his ministry.

The experience, example, and teaching of Jesus carried over into early Christian communities where women and men shared equally in the life and responsibilities of those communities. We know, however, that that equality changed in a rather short time. As the church became more and more mainstream, it began to adapt to the patriarchal structures of its own time. Part of this was the desire to conform in the face of persecution. It was dangerous business to appear radically unconventional. We can actually see this bias in the text. It shows up in the story of the early church as told in Acts, in the letters of Paul and as in our earlier reference to how Luke portrays women as always obedient. Biblical historians generally agree that later in its struggle against Gnosticism, the church lost or destroyed much of the written material from or about women.

As we look at these women who followed Jesus in his lifetime and after, we should be aware that what we see in the text hints at much more. What we have is what has survived, made it beyond the original bias, to be included and then beyond the later edits to remain. As scripture scholar, Elisabeth Moltmann–Wendel puts it:

> The tradition about women in the Jesus movement emerges from our Bible as no more than the tip of an iceberg. However, this tip is clearly visible, more clearly than in other corresponding documents of world literature…The Bible has within its pages a unique history of the greatness, the sovereignty, the wisdom and the courage of women. It is perhaps the most interesting book in connection with the emancipation of women. (The Women Around Jesus, *Elisabeth Moltmann-Wendel, Crossroad, New York, 1996, pp. 5-6).*

PRAYER OF THE
WOMEN WHO FOLLOWED JESUS

Soon afterwards he went on through cities and villages, proclaiming and bringing the good news of the kingdom of God. The twelve were with him, as well as some women who had been cured of evil spirits and infirmities: Mary, called Magdalene, from whom seven demons had gone out, and Joanna, the wife of Herod's steward Chuza, and Susanna, and many others, who provided for them out of their resources (Luke 8:1-3).

O God of all women who follow Jesus, we are grateful to be counted in that company.

We could not be there to walk the same ground, breathe the same air, see or hear first-hand.

But by your grace, we have heard the stories in your living Word.

By your grace, we've experienced His touch, His presence in our own lives as well.

Teach us by your Sons' words how to be faithful followers even as those first women were.

Guide us by your Son's example so that we, too, might live lives that witness to his message.

Heal us by your Son's presence with us here and now that we might become the women you formed us to be.

Amen

- KMcK

NEVER ON SUNDAY

A Look at the Women NOT in the Lectionary

WEEK NINE - THE WOMEN WHO FOLLOWED JESUS

Luke 8:1-3

1) *Read Mark 6:14-29, Luke 9:7-9, 13:31, 23:7-12. What does this tell you about the court of Herod where Joanna had resided and where her husband was the manager of the household? She is included as one of the women who had been cured of evil spirits or maladies. Most of Jesus' healings were met with thanksgiving and praise but Joanna went beyond that. Why do you think she chose to follow Jesus? What reaction do you imagine this had? How might she have served Jesus and his followers?*

2) *Read Matthew 20:20-24, 27:56, Mark 15:40-41, 16:1 James and John, this woman's sons, had been dubbed by Jesus, the "Sons of Thunder." They were among the inner circle of Jesus' apostles, there at the Transfiguration. Though Matthew later refers to Salome, who is thought to be the same woman, she is primarily identified by her relationship to the men in her life—wife of Zebedee, mother of James and John, mother of the sons of Zebedee. There is no mention of Zebedee on the scene. What circumstances of her life do you imagine prompted her to travel with Jesus and her sons? What kind of relationship might she have had with her sons? With Jesus? What growth do you see between the time she approaches Jesus in Mt 20 and where she stands in Mt 27 and where she goes in Mk 16:1 (as Salome)? Where are her sons then? Imagine her conversation with her "Sons of Thunder" afterward.*

3) *What surprises you as you look closely at these women? What questions does this raise for you?*

4)   *What do you think these women did, what role did they play after the Resurrection and in the earliest Judeo-Christian communities?*

5)   *What difference, if any, does it make to you to include women in Jesus' inner circle and/ or in roles of leadership?*

6)   *Choose one of the women in this group and write a Midrash to explain her following Jesus and her role in his ministry.*

CHALLENGE

Think of a woman in your own life—family, public figure, church, author, friend, whom you consider to be a faithful follower of Jesus. Identify what traits in her reveal Jesus to you. Write a letter to her. You can send it or not (sometimes letters to those no longer with us are the most significant). Prayerfully ask God to instill those same traits or gifts in you.

A CLOSER LOOK AT THE TEXT:
THE WOMEN WHO FOLLOWED JESUS

MARY, WIFE OF CLOPAS

Not much is known of this disciple but John places her at the foot of the cross along with Mary Magdalene, Mary the mother of Jesus, and Mary's sister, "standing near the cross of Jesus were his mother, and his mother's sister, Mary the wife of Clopas, and Mary Magdalene" (Jn 19:25). Her being there, however, speaks volumes. It identifies her as one of those who were the women disciples of Jesus and it attests to her faithfulness and closeness to Jesus that she was there at his death. Scholars speculate about her further identity. Some say this wife of Clopas is also Mary, the mother of James and John since they are never both listed at the same time. Others argue that the Clopas to whom she was married may be one and the same as the Cleopas on the road to Emmaus. The two names are not linguistically related—the Greek "Cleopas" and "Clopas" which is presumed to be Semitic. But grammarians say that such an interchange of names may have been a common occurrence. Identifying the wife of Clopas with the wife of Cleopas is not a majority opinion among scholars but it presents intriguing possibilities. The question then becomes, was this woman not only at the foot of the cross but was also the unnamed companion of Cleopas on the road to Emmaus? Might the two of them traveled together on foot from Jerusalem back to their home after "the things that have taken place there in these days" (Lk. 24:18). Might the two of them, as a married couple, have entreated Jesus to stay with them in their home and enjoyed with him the breaking of bread wherein they recognized him for who he was?

THE SISTER OF MARY

John's listing of the women at the foot of the cross is the first and only reference to a sister of Mary. As with "the brothers and sisters of Jesus," we cannot know from the use of the phrase if this refers to a sibling or a cousin. Either way it attests to the fact that Jesus had family ties and that among his first followers were these relatives.

It also opens up rich possibilities for consideration. For as much reflection as has been done on Mary, particularly within the Catholic and Orthodox traditions, little has been developed along the lines of Mary as the sister of another woman. It does speak, along with the episode with Elizabeth, to Mary's capacity to form strong, lasting bonds with other women. Perhaps you've had that experience as well.

MARY, THE MOTHER OF JAMES AND JOSES

Both Matthew and Mark list Mary, the mother of James among those at the cross (Luke does not provide names). All three synoptics list her among those who came to the tomb. (Luke's listing is after the fact in 24:10 when he says, "Now it was Mary Magdalene, Joanna, Mary the mother of James, and the other women with them who told this to the apostles." Because she is listed a few lines prior, she is likely the "other Mary" Matthew refers to: "Mary Magdalene and the other Mary were there, sitting opposite the tomb" (Mt. 27:61). This parallels Mark, "Mary Magdalene and Mary the mother of Joses saw where the body was laid" (Mk 15:47). (The abundance of Marys is confusing but remember that these were Miriam in Hebrew. Blame it on the popularity of our friend, Miriam, from the Hebrew Scriptures). Add to that confusion, the two James's. James, the brother of John, and son of Zebedee and Salome, is the one included in the triumvirate of Peter, James and John. They are invited by Jesus up the mountain to the Transfiguration and they are invited by him to the Garden of Gethsemane. This other James, of whom Mary is the mother, is sometimes referred to as James the Less as opposed to James the Great. Aside from making the distinction between this James and the other James included in the twelve apostles, there is much conjecture about James, the son of Mary. Is he also James, the son of Alpheus, (Mt 10:3, Mk 3:18, Lk 6:15, and Acts 1:13)? Is he the James, the brother of the Lord (Mt 13:55, Mk 6:3, Galatians 1:19, who was first Bishop of the Church of Jerusalem (Acts 15:21)? Most commentators are in agreement that such is the case. The relationship of his mother to others is made more complicated by this however. Does that make Mary, the mother of James, the same as the "sister of Mary" since James is the "brother of the Lord?"

SALOME, THE WIFE OF ZEBEDEE, THE MOTHER OF JAMES AND JOHN

Most scripture scholars take these three phrases to refer to the same woman. She is, therefore, present at both the foot of the cross and at the empty tomb. Mark refers to her as Salome:

"There were also women looking on from a distance; among them were Mary Magdalene, and Mary the mother of James the younger and of Joses, and Salome" (Mk 15:40),

"When the sabbath was over, Mary Magdalene, and Mary the mother of James, and Salome bought spices, so that they might go and anoint him" Mk. 16:1).

Matthew uses a nearly identical phrase having the women from Galilee looking on from a distance at the cross. But he identifies this woman by referencing her sons:

"Among them were Mary Magdalene, and Mary the mother of James and Joseph, and the mother of the sons of Zebedee" (Mt. 27:56).

This would mean that Salome, the mother of Zebedee's sons, was present at both the crucifixion and the tomb. It would mean that she was among the Galilean women following Jesus and was the one whose story is told as she approaches him in Mt 20:20-24. It would also mean that the later stories we have in Acts of her son, James, also affected her. As a follower of Jesus she would have heard him say, "ask, and it will be given you" (Mt 7:7) and, having come to believe in Jesus as Messiah, she spoke her heart's fondest desire to him—that her boisterous sons would be close to him, as partners with him, in the coming Kingdom. She may have remembered her request that they be at his left and his right as she stood at the cross and saw those crucified with him to his left and his right. Thankfully, she also had the first-hand experience of the Resurrection, the angel's words, "He has been raised; he is not here" Mk 16:6, to console her when her son, James, became the first of the twelve to be martyred. "About that time King Herod laid violent hands upon some who belonged to the church. He had James, the brother of John, killed with the sword. After he saw that it pleased the Jews, he proceeded to arrest Peter also" (Acts 12:1-3).

JOANNA, WIFE OF CHUZA

By reading the scripture passages that refer to Herod, particularly Mk 6:14-29, the beheading of John the Baptist, we get a glimpse of the world Joanna inhabited before Jesus came along and healed her. We do not know of what she was healed. We do not know of her relationship with Chuza, her husband whom she, presumably, left to follow Jesus (any more than we know of the relationship of Peter with his wife whom he also left for the same reason). Luke lists her as one who was at the grave and who gives witness to the empty tomb, "now it was Mary Magdalene, Joanna, Mary the mother of James, and the other women with them who told this to the apostles" (Lk 24:10). Luke does not provide a list of names for the crucifixion scene but only the phrase, "But all his acquaintances, including the women who had followed him from Galilee, stood at a distance, watching these things" (Lk 23:49). We can logically assume that Joanna was among that group who watched from a distance.

SUSANNA

Susanna is listed in Luke 8:1-3 as one of those women accompanying Jesus. As a group they are described as having been cured of evil spirits and infirmities and also as providing out of their resources. She is also, quite likely, one of the "others" referred to but not named at the crucifixion. These are the only specific things we know about Susanna—that and that her name has survived the transposition of centuries. All in all, no small feat and much to be known for.

MARY THE MOTHER OF JESUS
See Week Seven

MARY MAGDALENE
See Week Ten

MEANWHILE, ON SUNDAY MORNING....

The listing by name in Luke of the women who followed Jesus, Lk.8:1-3 is never read on a Sunday morning. It is the Gospel reading for Friday of the Twenty-Fourth Week of the Year (#447).

MARY MAGDALENE
AT THE
TOMB

BACKGROUND:
MARY MAGDALENE AT THE TOMB

Mary of Magdala, or Mary Magdalene, is named 14 times in the Gospels, more than any of the disciples outside of Peter, James, and John. This, of itself, is remarkable when we cannot even get a list of the 12 names of the apostles that "match." (Mark and Matthew list a "Thaddeus" who is, presumably, the same person listed in Luke as "Judas, son of James." John uses the name "Nathaniel" where the synoptics use "Bartholomew"). Even more important, however, than the frequency with which her name appears, is the time and place of her appearance. All four gospels place Mary Magdalene at both the crucifixion and the resurrection—the only one so named. This establishes, beyond a doubt, not only her historical presence at these central events in the life of Christ, but it is also an indication of her importance—both in the life of the followers of Jesus and in the life of the early church that recorded these events.

In being sent by Jesus to bear the news of his resurrection (Jn 20:11-19), Mary becomes "Apostle to the Apostles"—a phrase first coined by Hippolytus of Rome in the second century. According to Webster, the word "apostle" means "one sent on a mission." In these passages, it is Jesus himself who sends her with the most essential mission or message—that He is risen, and he sends her to the most critical of persons—his innermost followers. "Apostle" is a title of great distinction in the Bible. Paul would later make a great deal of what it means to be an apostle, "Last of all he was seen by me, as one born out of the normal course. I am the least of the apostles; in fact, because I persecuted the church of God, I do not even deserve the name. But by God's favor I am what I am" (1Cor. 15:9-10) and he would roundly condemn false prophets. But Mary Magdalene lives up to every definition of apostle—be that of Hippolytus, Paul or Webster. And that claim is based entirely and legitimately on what is found in scripture.

She is sent with authority on a mission. She is the first to proclaim the news of the risen Lord. Her news, "I have seen the Lord!" is the central message of Christianity. As Paul would later write, "If Christ has not been raised, then empty is our preaching; empty, too your faith." (1 Cor. 15:14) She is eyewitness to both the resurrection of Christ and to the example of his life lived among us.

Without the witness of Mary Magdalene and the other women who stood at the cross and came to the tomb we would have no first-hand account of Easter. We would not know what happened. Jesus chose to entrust her with the most important of proclamations. In addition to being a witness to the resurrection, Mary of Magdala is a faithful disciple for all the time she spent supporting Jesus throughout his ministry and sharing his life and that of his followers.

PETER AND MARY

Peter was present at the Transfiguration and saw Jesus in his glory (Mt 17:1-4, Mk 9:2-6, Lk 9:28-36).	Mary was present at the Crucifixion and saw Jesus in his agony (Mt 27:56, Mk 15:40, Jn 19:25).
Peter heard the heavens proclaim Jesus son of God at his baptism by John (Mt 17:5, Mk 9:7, Lk 9:35).	Mary heard Jesus cry out that God had forsaken him (Mt 27:46, Mk 15:34).
Peter "left everything" to follow Jesus (Mt 19:27, Mk 10:28, Lk 18:28).	Mary provided for Jesus out of her means (Lk 8L1-3).
After denying him 3 times (Mt 26:58-75), Mk 14L54-72, Lk 18:28), Peter was given 3 chances to proclaim his love for Jesus (Jn 21:15-17).	Mary was healed of seven demons (Lk 8:2).
Peter slept in the Garden of Gethsemane (Mt 26:37-46, Mk 14:33-42).	Mary encountered Jesus in the Garden at the tomb (Jn 20:11-17, Mk 16:9).
After seeing the empty tomb, Peter "went back home" (Jn 20:10).	After seeing the empty tomb, Mary stayed and encountered Jesus. (Jn 20:11-18).
The angel told the women to go and tell Peter of Jesus' resurrection (Mk 16:7).	Mary was told by Jesus to "go to my brothers" (Jn 20:17).

PRAYER OF
MARY MAGDALENE AT THE TOMB

Meanwhile, Mary stood weeping beside the tomb. Even as she wept, she stooped to peer inside, and there she saw two angels in dazzling robes. One was seated at the head and the other at the foot of the place where Jesus' body had lain. "Woman," they asked her, "why are you weeping?" She answered them, "Because the Lord has been taken away, and I do not know where they have put him." She had no sooner said this than she turned around and caught sight of Jesus standing there. But she did not know him. "Woman," he asked her, "why are you weeping? Who is it you are looking for?" She supposed he was the gardener, so she said, "Sir, if you are the one who carried him off, tell me where you have laid him and I will take him away." Jesus said to her, "Mary!" She turned to him and said [in Hebrew], "Rabbouni!" (meaning "Teacher"). Jesus then said: "Do not cling to me, for I have not yet ascended to the Father. Rather, go to my brothers and tell them, 'I am ascending to my Father and your Father, to my God and your God!'" Mary Magdalene went to the disciples. "I have seen the Lord!" she announced. Then she reported what he had said to her. (Jn 20:11-18)

Rabbouni,

You call us by our name

And our hearts leap within us.

Can it be that you are alive—so close, so real?

Darkness and death are scattered in the light of your being

And we dare to believe.

We want to hold this moment, hold you forever.

Yet you would have us carry our new-found belief to others. It is your trust in us that sends us in your name.

We bear the news that you are alive!

That everything is now changed and made new in you. We cannot contain it!

The joy spills and spirals out until we hear our own words echoing back, "I have seen the Lord!"

May our lives proclaim to all whom we meet that you are alive and in our midst.

Amen.

- KMcK

NEVER ON SUNDAY
A Look at the Women NOT in the Lectionary

WEEK TEN - MARY MAGDALENE AT THE TOMB

John 20:11-18:

1) *Last week in Luke 8:1-3, Mary Magdalene was listed among the women accompanying and traveling with Jesus as, "Mary called the Magdalene, from whom seven devils had gone out"(Lk. 8:2). Make a quick check of some of these other scripture references to demon possession: a)Mt 8:28-34 OR Mk 5:1-10 OR Lk 8:26-38, b) Mt 9:32-34, c) Mt 12:22-24 OR Lk 11:14-16, d) Mt 17:14-18 OR Lk 9:37-44, e)Lk 4:33-37, f) Mt 15:21- 28 OR Mk 7:24-30 Are any of these possessions associated with sinfulness?*

2) *Compare the "Peter and Mary" side by side, p. 74. In what ways are the experiences that Peter and Mary had of Jesus similar? In what ways are they different?*

3) *All four gospels place Mary Magdalene at the scene of the Resurrection. Only John has the touching scene between Mary and Jesus in the garden. What details of that scene touch your imagination? Raise questions for you?*

4) *What do you think the exchange is about where Jesus says, "Do not hold on to me, because I have not yet ascended to the Father"? Is it more understandable in the context of the next line, "But go to my brothers and say to them…"?*

5) *In John 20:11:18, Mary encounters the risen Lord. She is sent to announce to the others that Jesus has risen from the dead. St. Augustine wrote of Mary Magdalene in the fourth century, "The Holy Spirit made Magdalene the Apostle of the Apostles." Is that how you have commonly thought of, or pictured, Mary Magdalene? Why or why not?*

6) *Mary Magdalene has inspired much artwork—paintings, poetry, etc. Try looking some up and notice how she is portrayed. What questions does this raise? Compare your findings and reactions with the other women in your group.*

CHALLENGE

Mary is confused about who she encounters in the garden, thinking Jesus is the gardener. Then he calls her by name and she recognizes him. Is there a time in your life when, out of the confusion, you have heard Jesus call you by name? What moved within you? What was your response?

A CLOSER LOOK AT THE TEXT:
MARY MAGDALENE AT THE TOMB

So far we have looked only to the gospels for our information on Mary Magdalene. How do we account for the "other" images of her? She has been portrayed frequently in the past as a great sinner—standing in scarlet contrast, as it were, to the virginal blue of Mary, Jesus' mother. More recently she has taken center stage in the DaVinci Code and popular lore as the par armor of Jesus. How did all this happen? Who was she really?

Despite the teachings of the Early Church Fathers who frequently extolled the virtues of Mary Magdalene, over time a different picture of her emerged. Some of this can be attributed to confusion over the several Marys and other women of the gospels and the resulting tendency to conflate these into one. In 590 A.D., Pope Gregory the Great preached a homily in which he combined the woman who anointed Jesus in Luke's gospel with Mary of Bethany and Mary of Magdala. Using allegory, he equated the seven demons of the gospel with the seven deadly sins and said, "She whom Luke calls the sinful woman, whom John calls Mary, we believe to be the Mary from whom seven devils were ejected according to Mark. And what did these seven devils signify, if not all the vices?" She thus became a model of repentance rather than a model of discipleship. She actually became named the Patron Saint of Prostitutes, a far cry from Apostle to the Apostles. Artists, writers and commentators found much to mine in this salacious image. To this day the image of Mary Magdalene is commonly that of a great sinner—one who has repented, to be sure, but one whose past is full of sin, usually sexual sin, at that.

The recent popularization of Mary Magdalene vis a vis the DaVinci Code capitalizes on the way in which Mary was "demoted" by the Church. Though this was more likely due to ignorance and poor scholarship than to intention, the fact remains that Mary's importance was lost over time. To that we add the rather recent re-discovery of old manuscripts. The Dead Sea Scrolls that we visited early in our year were discovered in

Israel in 1947. Two years previous, in 1945, in near Nag Hammadi in Upper Egypt, a similar cache of texts was found that dated back to a somewhat later period in the early Christian era. Commonly referred to as the Gnostic Gospels, these represent writings that are contemporary to, or shortly after, the Gospels of Mark, Matthew, Luke and John. While the writings at Nag Hammadi were not the only Gnostic Gospels around, they were extensive and well preserved. They also brought to the public awareness the existence of other non-canonical "gospels" written about the life of Christ. These writings shed fascinating light on the life of Christianity in its early, formative stages. As such they are a great resource for our understanding. In these other "gospels" are intriguing passages about Mary Magdalene that portray her as favored by Jesus, as a leader in the early Church and as one in conflict with Peter. These provide the basis for the recent upsurge of interest in and speculation about Mary of Magdala.

So, what do we make of these other "gospels?" Very likely, these were available, along with many others, when the Canon of the New Testament was put together but they were not included. According to the Jerome Biblical Commentary, the criteria for preserving and accepting the Christian writings that were to become our New Testament were: 1) apostolic origins, real or reputed, 2) addressed to particular Christian communities, 3) conformity with Christian doctrine. About those "gospels" not included, the commentary writes:

> Alongside the four Gospels, oral and written material from the 1st century seems to have survived into the 2nd century and even later. Some of this was incorporated into apocryphal gospels. The apocryphal Gospel of Thomas contains sayings of Jesus that may well be authentic. How many of these apocryphal gospels existed in the 2nd century we do not know, but in his first homily on Luke, Origen mentions that many had attempted to write gospels (he names five) but had not been guided by the Spirit. Origen, of course, wrote at a time when four and only four Gospels were accepted, but was it thus during the 2nd century? Were some of the gospels now considered apocryphal used by certain communities as their gospels even as the canonical Gospels were used by their respective communities? (Vol. II, p. 528).

In today's world of contemporary biblical scholarship and with resources that were never dreamed of in the days of Pope Gregory, there is no reason to perpetuate the false notion of Mary Magdalene as penitent sinner. Nor do we need to look any farther than the Mary of the Gospels to claim her importance. In the face of overwhelming evidence to the contrary, it is irresponsible to continue to cast Mary Magdalene as a prostitute or sinner. It also robs us of the powerful witness of a remarkable woman of faith, a partner with Jesus in the Good News and the herald of the resurrection.

MEANWHILE, ON SUNDAY MORNING....

John's Resurrection story is told in two scenes. In 20:1-10, Mary Magdalene encountered the empty tomb and ran to tell the disciples. Peter and "the beloved disciple" ran with her back to the tomb to see what she saw and then returned home. In Jn 20:11-18, Mary has the subsequent encounter with the risen Jesus. The first scene is read on Easter in every one of the three cycles, the second scene is never read on Easter Sunday, or any Sunday, even within the Octave of Easter. It is only read on the Tuesday of the Week following Easter. (N.B. This is only true of the Roman Lectionary; the Easter reading includes vs 11-18 in the other lectionaries—the Revised Common Lectionary, the Episcopal, the Lutheran and the United Methodist. Also worthy of note: the Canadian Roman Lectionary has been revised to include these passages but the American was not).

WOMEN
IN THE
EARLY CHURCH
I

BACKGROUND:
WOMEN IN THE EARLY CHURCH, I

Just as we learned the various strands of oral tradition and authorship that came together to create the Hebrew Scriptures, it is helpful to see how the New Testament came to be. The timeline that follows helps place some of the significant events and documents of the early Church in those years after Jesus' death and resurrection.

There was no imperative in the early church to write down what had happened. The model we see in the Acts of the Apostles and in Paul's letters is of the message of Jesus spreading by word of mouth and of communities of faith springing up. The first writings are Paul's letters to these early communities that he had been instrumental in establishing. When the first Christians gathered to remember and tell the stories of Jesus and to share a Eucharistic meal, the scripture that they shared was the Hebrew psalms, prayers and other readings. Paul's letters quickly became a fixture at their gathering as well and were shared among the communities.

Paul was a Pharisee educated in Jerusalem by Rabbi Gamaliel (Acts 26:5). He never knew Jesus in person but encountered the Risen Lord in a dramatic event on the road to Damascus that changed his life—one that changed him from persecutor to apostle. From 46-58 he traveled throughout Asia Minor and Greece preaching the gospel. He made many Gentile converts and, thus, made the early church address the relationship of Gentile to Jewish Christians—the first issue at the Jerusalem Council of 49. Paul's first missionary journey, 46-49, was through Cyprus and Asia Minor, described in Acts 13-14. His second mission, 49-52, took him to Asia Minor, Troas, Macedonia and Greece. It was on this journey that he wrote his first letter to one of the churches he'd founded on the earlier trip, the First Letter to the Thessalonians. On his third missionary journey, 54-57, he traveled through Northern Galatia and Phrygia to Ephesus. In all cases he evangelized then established local communities with leaders to care for the new believers. He went on writing to all his converts from the various other locations. In 58, he was arrested in Jerusalem and remained in house arrest in Caesarea for two years before being sent to Rome for trial. He was martyred in Rome in 67. Several of his letters were written while he was in captivity. Other letters attributed to Paul were actually written by his disciples, in his name—some of them after his death.

At first the early Christians expected that Christ's return, the *parousia*, was imminent. We can see traces of that in the earliest of Paul's letter to the Thessalonians. Over time Christians realized that the parousia would not happen in their lifetime and, thus, the writing down of what had been learned became important to preserve for future generations. The first of these gospels was Mark's written about 65. Later both Matthew and Luke would write down their versions. In so doing, they each drew from what Mark has written, their own resources, and a body of shared information that scripture scholars have named "Q" for *quelle* or "source." Each evangelist wrote for their own purposes with a particular community in mind. The Gospel of Luke is actually the first half of a two-part accounting. In the Acts of the Apostles, he continues the story of Jesus to include the story of the early Church.

The Gospel of John would not be written until much later, some time in the 90's. Aware of the other gospels, John writes in a completely different, style, tone, and setting. Attributed to the "beloved disciple," first-hand witness to the life of Jesus, scholars debate whether this was, indeed, written by John, one of the twelve, or a text written by the Johanine community that formed around him. In either case, the Gospel of John is not a simple story line but, rather, a mature and complex Christological statement.

EVENTS AND WRITINGS OF THE EARLY CHURCH

28-30	Public ministry of Jesus
30	Passion, death and Resurrection of Jesus
36	Martyrdom of Stephen / Conversion of Paul
46-49	Paul's first missionary journey
49	**First Jerusalem Council**
50	**Martyrdom of James**
49-52	Paul's second missionary journey
	Paul's first (and second) letters to the Thessalonians
54-57	Paul's third missionary journey
	Paul's letter to the Galatians
	Paul's letter to the Philippians
	Paul's first and second letter to the Corinthians
	Paul's letter to the Romans
58-60	Paul imprisoned in Caesarea
61-63	Paul imprisoned in Rome Paul's letter to
	Philomen Paul's letter to the Colossians
	"Paul's" letter to the Ephesians
	"Paul's" letters to Timothy and Titus
67	**Martyrdom of Paul**
c. 65-70	Gospel of Mark
c. 80	First Letter of Peter
c. 80	**Martyrdom of Peter**
c. 75-85	Letter to the Hebrews c. 80 – Letter of "James"
c. 80-85	Gospel of Matthew
c. 80-85	Gospel of Luke / Acts of the Apostles
c. 80-90	Letter of "Jude"
90's	Gospel of John I, II, III John Revelation
c.100	Second Letter of Peter

PRAYER OF
THE WOMEN IN THE EARLY CHURCH, I

Jesus of Nazareth,

the stories we hear of you are almost too good to be true. You recognize us as women;

You recognize us as worthy of bearing your name and your mission. Such trust engenders great joy and willingness in our hearts.

What is there we would not do for You?

We rejoice in those women who faithfully heard and responded to your invitation.

Fill us with that same devotion and zeal to follow You and to bring others to follow You as well.

Inspired by your confidence in us, may we overcome whatever limitations we have placed on ourselves or received from others. We thank you and call you our Savior and Lord.

You have made us worthy in your sight.

You have entrusted us with the sacred task of being your partners in building the kingdom. What joy!

Amen

- KMcK

NEVER ON SUNDAY
A Look at the Women NOT in the Lectionary

WEEK ELEVEN
WOMEN IN THE EARLY CHURCH, I

Acts 9: 36-42, 12:12, 16:11-15,40

1) *Acts 9:36-42. Tabitha, or Dorcas, is the first woman to be named in Acts. Her healing resembles that of the daughter of Jairus in Mark 5: 35-43. Notice that vs. 36 introduces her as "a disciple whose name was Tabitha, which in Greek is Dorcas." This is the first and only example of a woman being so specifically identified, i.e. with the feminine form of the noun disciple. Her works of charity endeared her to others and preserved her name throughout the ages. What women like her have you known in your life whose works of charity have endeared them to you and to others and have preserved their names throughout the ages?*

2) *As soon as he realized this, he went to the house of Mary, the mother of John whose other name was Mark, where many had gathered and were praying (Acts 12:12). Read the larger pericope, Chapter 12, the story of Peter's imprisonment and escape. Why does Peter immediately go to her home? What do you think is the significance of this early gathering of Jesus' followers in Mary's home? Imagine who might be gathered inside, worried about Peter. What would there reaction be to the flustered Rhoda? Check your footnotes for clues on the identities of the persons named. Share your findings with your group. What women have you known who are at the center, making connections, building up the kingdom?*

3) *Read the story of Lydia, Acts 16:11-15, within it's larger setting of Acts 16:1-40. Again, pay close attention to your footnotes for details to share with your group. In crossing over to Macedonia, Paul, and with him the early church, first steps foot in Europe. In searching*

for a worshiping Jewish community he happens upon Lydia and the other women and sits down to speak with them. What questions does this raise for you? Was this what you expected of Paul? What does it mean that she is a "worshipper of God?" She is one of the few women in Luke's writings who actually speaks in vs. 15. What do you find significant in her words? Notice Lydia's hospitality in both vs. 15 and vs. 40. What does this tell you about her and her household? Paul followed his usual pattern and established a church there in Philippi. Apparently, it flourished— "I am confident of this, that the one who began a good work among you will bring it to completion by the day of Jesus Christ" (Philippians 6:1). How do you think this "church" grew from its beginnings with Lydia? What women have you known who've used their gifts of hospitality and leadership to build community or create something new?

4) *Write a Midrash as one of women in these above pericopes.*

CHALLENGE

Consider the role of women in the Church as you were growing up and as you see it today. Did you ever have a sense that it was once different? That it could be different? What would you want for the women of tomorrow? Spend some time this week in prayer on these questions. Pray for those in leadership—both men and women.

A CLOSER LOOK AT THE TEXT:
WOMEN IN THE EARLY CHURCH, I

TABITHA OR DORCAS – ACTS 9:36-42

This story is the first chronologically of all the ones we are looking at, coming very early in Acts, chapter nine, while the church was still very young. It bears a striking resemblance to the story in Mark 5 of Jesus raising the daughter of Jairus. Even the words Peter speaks, *"Tabitha, rise up,"* echo the Aramaic words we hear from Jesus, *"Talitha, kuom"* (Mk 5:41) meaning, "little girl, get up." Like the story from Mark, this speaks to the miraculous power of relationships for, in each one, it is the intercession of others that precipitates the miracle. It also confirms, early in Acts as it is, that Peter has been given the power, through Christ, to heal as Christ did.

This miracle story is often overshadowed by the story of Cornelius that follows—both the vision Peter receives and the conversion of Cornelius and his household. It deserves its own consideration, however. We see here one of the earliest references to widows performing a specific function within the church, and we see it very early on. There ended up being three specific roles within the church that were professed, enrolled or consecrated—virgins, widows, and deacons. These were somewhat fluid roles and at this early stage are only beginning to take shape but here we see it attested to. This pericope provides us with an insight, however, into that world. This is not a story of almsgiving in the sense of passing out crumbs from the table of the rich. Rather, Tabitha has poured herself into her good works, creating products of her own hands—by her labor rather than her wealth. This, it seems, was greatly esteemed by her community. She is explicitly described as a disciple devoted to good works which attests to her being long remembered in the community because of the way she gave other people life by her good works. Nor was she esteemed only by the women of the community for it is two of the men who summon Peter (vs. 38).

MARY, MOTHER OF JOHN MARK – ACTS 12:12

Mary was the mother of John Mark, a co-worker of Paul and an aunt or cousin of Barnabas. We see here that she knew Peter but, because of her son, she probably had some connection with Paul as well. We read, quite early in Acts, about Peter seeking refuge in Mary's house after his miraculous freeing from prison. *After coming to realize this, he went to the house of Mary, the mother of John (also known as Mark). (Acts 12:12).*

This is followed by a somewhat comical scene wherein Mary's maid **Rhoda** answers Peter's knocking at the door and is so flustered to see him there that she leaves him standing outside as she flees inside with the news. What is noteworthy here is that it is to Mary's home that Peter went. Her house seems to have been the place where these early Christians gathered to pray and to seek refuge when necessary.

LYDIA – ACTS 16:11-15

In this Closer Look at Lydia, we will employ one of the tools of biblical scholarship known as **redaction criticism**. Redaction criticism is related to editing and studies the original language of the text. It examines words very closely for the idiosyncrasies of spelling, comparing it to other words of similar meaning, etc. A redactic scholar would point out, for example, that in the changing of Abram to Abraham and the changing of Sarai to Sarah, we have the introduction, in each case, of the H that is part of the acronym for God's holy, unspeakable name. Thus, it is an indication of how both Abraham and Sarah are now totally given over to YHWH.

Some of the details of this pericope about Lydia reveal to us that she was originally from Thyatira and that she was a "worshipper of God," a "God-fearer," or, as in the NAB, she "reverenced God." This phrase refers to Gentiles attracted to Judaism, those persons who are not Jewish but who worship the God of the Jews.

Exegetes have traditionally looked at Lydia's conversion story as the prelude to the jailer's conversion (and the slave girl's exorcism as setting the stage for that). Yet Lydia's conversion is founded on a receptive heart, "she already reverenced God," and a willing response, "The Lord opened her heart to hear what Paul was saying." The jailer's conversion, on the other hand, was largely motivated by fear.

Let's hone in, for a moment, on that opening scene, vs. 13: *"Once, on the Sabbath, we went outside the city gate to the bank of the river, where we thought there would be a place of prayer. We sat down and spoke to the women who were gathered there."* Ivoni Richter Reimer, a Brazilian liberation theologian, offers a surgically precise text criticism of this periscope that allows us to discover much more than meets the eye.

She looks first to the Greek verb, συνέρχεσθαι, "to gather" and explores every other reference in the New Testament (e.g. John 18:20 when Jesus says, "I always taught in a synagogue or in the temple area where all the Jews come together")—texts that use that particular form of the verb, and she comes to the conclusion that whenever συνέρχεσθαι is used, it is an intentional gathering that also implies community. She then looks at the verb for "sit down," καθίζειν and finds that it is a form specifically connected with teaching and preaching—as in Lk 4:21 when after reading in the synagogue, Jesus sat down to interpret what he'd read. She looks, then, at the third verb, λαλεῖν, meaning "to speak." Here again she finds specific contexts for this verb wherein it is particularly related to preaching in the synagogue or Temple. After looking at the three verbs, she turns her attention to the word, προσευχή, which indentifies the gathering place. Unlike the three verbs this noun has received much attention, largely debating whether it means "synagogue" or "house of prayer." Either interpretation, added to the enhanced rendering of the verbs, leads to the same conclusion. Reimer offers this tantalizing summary:

> It appears from the word analysis above that the missionaries spent their Sabbath in the same way as in other places where, according to their custom, they participated in Jewish worship. We are talking about a liturgical action that presumed the existence of a Jewish community in the place. The missionaries only participate and if they had not been there, the liturgical action would have been carried out by someone else in that place, as usual. The difficulty in giving an "unproblematic" reading of this account lies, in my opinion, in the fact that the text speaks here of a gathering of women (Women in the Acts of the Apostles, *Ivoni Richter Reimer, p. 78*).

She then goes on to say after exploring the arguments for Luke's choice of words:

> The best answer to the speculative proposals mentioned above seems to be that Luke's report rests on a source and that it transmits the content of the source virtually without alteration. According to this source, then, women were gathered on the Sabbath in the synagogue at Philippi and the missionaries, after seating themselves, interpreted scripture for them. But although this statement of the text corresponds to the circumstances of the period [Reimer goes on to prove its plausibility], may exegetes have difficulty with it. They assert that if only women were gathered, this could not have been a synagogue in which divine worship is celebrated. (Women in the Acts of the Apostles, *Ivoni Richter Reimer, p. 91*).

We will encounter this kind of logic again before we are done.

Another redactic insight comes in the wording in vs. 15 when Lydia "prevailed" upon Paul to come to her home. It is the same verb used in Lk 24:29 when the disciples on the road to Emmaus press Jesus to stay with them. Lydian calls upon the authenticity of her new baptism when she says, *"If you are convinced that I believe in the Lord, come and stay at my house."* The conviction of her argument and her hospitality win Paul over and later when he is released from prison he returns to the safety of her home, much as Peter went to Mary the mother of John Mark. It is there where the others are gathered, even as they had in Mary's Jerusalem home.

Lydia is the first European in scripture to be converted to Christianity. The house church that began with in Philippi in her home grew to become a community that Paul wrote back to with great affection and praise. *"I am sure of this much: that he who has begun the good work in you will carry it through to completion, right up to the day of Christ Jesus"* (Philippians 1:6). Paul's mission there began with women and we have every reason to believe they remained important. We have further proof of that later in the same letter as Paul urges two women leaders to reconcile.

Commentators have for years used Lydia's description as a "dealer in purple goods" to indicate that she was a wealthy merchant, connected with the upper class. Newer research, however, particularly on the trade of dyeing and on Philippian culture, yields contradictory information. Dyeing was a messy trade that left the skin permanently stained and a smelly one that was typically done outside of the city because of its offensive odor. Those who plied the trade were usually women, slaves and freed persons, persons who lived outside of the polite society. Indeed, the fact that Lydia has no "proper name," i.e. a designation of her by city or by husband's name, indicates that she was in a low socioeconomic class.

It may not matter what Lydia's economic status was. She is a woman of leadership, power and persuasion either way—rather that is among the wealthy or among the poor. We are graced to have her words preserved in scripture, words that speak with authority about the depth of her faith. She is whole-hearted in her acceptance of Christianity and of Paul and willingly opens her life and home regardless of the consequences. Her initial example took root and gave life to an extraordinary Christian community.

MEANWHILE, ON SUNDAY MORNING....

In the weeks following Easter the lectionary recounts the story of the early church in Acts. The story of Tabitha or Dorcas is read on Saturday of the Third Week of Easter and the story of Lydia is told on Monday of the Sixth Week of Easter. Mary of Jerusalem and her servant, Rhoda, are not included in these weekday readings.

WOMEN
IN THE
EARLY CHURCH
II

BACKGROUND:
WOMEN IN THE EARLY CHURCH, II

WOMEN OF ROMANS 16

I commend to you our sister, Phoebe, who is a deacon of the church of Cenchreae. Please welcome her in the Lord, as saints should. If she needs help in anything, give it to her for she herself has been a benefactor to many, including myself. Give my greetings to Prisca and Aquila; they were my fellow workers in the service of Christ Jesus and even risked their lives for me. Not only I but all the churches of the Gentiles are grateful to them. Remember me also to the congregation that meets in their house. Greetings to my beloved Eaenetus; he is the first offering that Asia made to Christ. My greetings to Mary, who has worked hard for you, and to Andronicus and Junia, my kinsmen and fellow prisoners; they are outstanding apostles, and they were in Christ even before I was. Greetings to Ampliatus, who is dear to me in the Lord; to Urbanus, our fellow worker in the service of Christ; and to my beloved Stachys. Greetings to Apelles, who proved himself in Christ's service, and to all who belong to the household of Aritobulus. Greetings to my kinsman Herodion and to the member of the household of Narcissus who are in the Lord. Greetings, too, to Tryphaena and Tryphosa, who have worked hard for the Lord; and also to dear Persis, who has labored long in the Lord's service. Greetings to Rufus, a chosen servant of the Lord, and to his mother, who has been a mother to me as well. Greetings to Asyncritus, Phlegon, Hermes, Patrobas, Hermas, and the brothers who are with them; to Philiolgus and Julia, to Nereus and his sister, to Olympas, and all the saints who are with them. (Romans 16:1-15)

Phoebe
Prisca
Mary
Junia
Tryphaena

Tryphosa
Persis
Mother of Rufus
Julia
Sister of Nereus.

Paul, who has not yet been to Rome, sends greetings, by way of Phoebe, to all of those known to be prominent in the church in Rome. Of the 28 people named, 10 of them are women (36%). We have already learned the significance of a woman's name being preserved in the sacred text. Several of these appear later but all are worthy of being named here to honor their memory and their role in founding the first church of Rome. There is nothing in Paul's greeting that differentiates between the status or ministry of the women from the men.

APPHIA - COLOSSAE

Paul, a prisoner for Christ Jesus, and Timothy our brother, to our beloved friend and fellow worker Philemon, to Apphia our sister, to our fellow soldier Archippus, and to the church that meets in your house. (Philemon vs. 2)

Apphia presided with two others, Philemon and Achippus, as leaders of a house church in Colossae

CHLOE - CORINTH

For it has been reported to me by Chloe's people that there are quarrels among you, my brothers and sisters (I Cor. 1:11).

This is the only time Chloe is mentioned but the phrase "Chloe's people" refers to the members of Chloe's household. Most likely this included many beyond the immediate family. It would have been typical in the ancient world for the household to have included her slaves, freed-persons, or dependent workers as well as extended family. Since all of these persons are identified by her name, this suggests that Chloe was the head of the household. This gives us a clue of Chloe's status in society at large and, possibly, also within the Corinthian Christian community.

CLAUDIA - ROME

This letter is written while Paul is in prison in Rome. At this point, he is without hope of release; he expects to be condemned soon and to suffer martyrdom in the near future. Thus its tone takes on special significance and endearment.

Get here before winter if you can. Eubulus, Pudens, Linus, Claudia, and all the brothers send greetings. (2 Tim. 4:21)

Paul entreats Timothy to come and sends greetings to him from himself and from his fellow Christians. Claudia is identified in early Christian tracts as the mother of Linus, the successor of Peter as Bishop of Rome.

DAMARIS - ATHENS

A few did join him, however, to become believers. Among these were Dionysius, a member of the court of the Areopagus, a woman named Damaris, and a few others. (Acts 17:34)

Paul's attempts to evangelize the Athenians are, for the most part, politely but firmly rejected—only two, in fact, are named and one of these is a woman, Damaris.

LOIS AND EUNICE, GRANDMOTHER AND MOTHER OF TIMOTHY - LYSTRA

I recall your sincere faith that first lived in your grandmother Lois and in your mother Eunice and that I am confident lives also in you. (2Tim. 1:5)

But you, remain faithful to what you have learned and believed, because you know from whom you learned it, and that from infancy you have known [the] sacred scriptures, which are capable of giving you wisdom for salvation through faith in Christ Jesus. (2 Tim. 3:14-15)

Paul reached Derbe and Lystra where there was a disciple named Timothy, the son of a Jewish woman who was a believer, but his father was a Greek. The brothers in Lystra and Iconium spoke highly of him, and Paul wanted him to come along with him. On account of the Jews of that region, Paul had him circumcised, for they all knew that his father was a Greek. (Acts 16:1-3)

Timothy is an important and beloved disciple of Paul, the one that, above, he entreats to come join him. It is significant that Paul attributes Timothy's education to his grandmother and mother. There are several implications in the statement that these women were responsible for passing on the legacy of reading and teaching the Scriptures to the young Timothy. They must have been fairly well educated themselves, able to read, to interpret, and to teach. They must have believed that the Gospel they received from Paul and Barnabas was consistent and continuous with the Old Testament, for that was their Scripture.

EUODIA AND SYNTYCHE - PHILIPPI

I urge Euodia and I urge Syntyche to come to a mutual understanding in the Lord. Yes, and I ask you also, my true yokemate, to help them for they have struggled at my side in promoting the gospel, along with Clement and my other co-workers, whose names are in the book of life. (Phil. 4:2-3)

This is from Paul's letter to the Philippians, the community that he founded while with Lydia. The very fact of Paul's expressed concern over their disagreement suggests that these two women held positions of prominence in the community—that the whole community knew them and knew the basis of their dispute, unnamed here by Paul. So, women continued to play leadership roles in the church at Philippi.

PRISCILLA - ROME, CORINTH, EPHESUS

After that, Paul left Athens and went to Corinth. There he found a Jew named Aquila, a native of Pontus recently arrived from Italy with his wife Priscilla. An edict of Claudius had ordered all Jews to leave Rome. Paul went to visit the pair, whose trade he had in common with them. He took up lodgings with them and they worked together as tentmakers. (Acts 18:1-3)

Paul stayed on in Corinth for quite a while; but eventually he took leave of the brothers and sailed for Syria, in the company of Priscilla and Aquila.. At the port of Cenchreae he shaved his head because of a vow he had taken. When they landed at Ephesus, he left Priscilla and Aquila behind and entered the synagogue to hold discussions with the Jews. (Acts 18:18-19)

A Jew named Apollos, a native of Alexandria and a man of eloquence, arrived by ship at Ephesus. He was both an authority on Scripture and instructed in the new way of the Lord. Apollos was a man full of spiritual fervor. He spoke and taught accurately about Jesus, although he knew only of John's baptism. He too began to express himself fearlessly in the synagogue. When Priscilla and Aquila heard him, they took him home and explained to him God's new way in greater detail. (Acts 18:24-26)

Give my greetings to Prisca and Aquila; they were my fellow workers in the service of Christ Jesus and even risked their lives for the sake of mine. Not only I but all the churches of the Gentiles are grateful to them. (Rom. 16:3-4)

The churches of Asia send you greetings. Aquila and Prisca, together with the assembly that meets in their house, send you cordial greetings in the Lord. (1 Cor. 16:19)

Greet Prisca and Aquila and the family of Onesiphorus. (2 Tim. 4:19)

Because we have Priscilla referenced several times, appearing in both Paul's writings and in Luke's Acts, we know quite a bit about her and her husband, Aquila. Of these several listings, Priscilla is listed first more often thus indicating that she was the more important of the two—she is certainly not included in the text simply as Aquila's wife.

JUNIA - ROME

My greetings to Mary, who has worked hard for you, and to Andronicus and Junia, my kinsmen and fellow prisoners; they are outstanding apostles, and they were in Christ even before I was. (Romans 16:7)

PRAYER OF
THE WOMEN IN THE EARLY CHURCH, II

We thank you, Lord, for the example of these holy women.

We thank you that you entrusted to them the building up of your church.

May we be as faithful in teaching, serving, encouraging and in spreading the word of your Kingdom.

It is too easy, Lord, to think it was once simpler or better.

We are the women you choose to use today.

We are born in this time and this place that we might make it holy, that we might bring about your Kingdom in the here and now.

Nor would you ask us anything without gifting us for the task. Stir within us the confidence to act in your name.

Inspire within us a great desire to know you, to follow you and to share your love with others.

May the Church you love be made better and more faithful to your vision by receiving the gifts we offer.

Amen.

- KMcK

NEVER ON SUNDAY
A Look at the Women NOT in the Lectionary

WEEK TWELVE
WOMEN IN THE EARLY CHURCH, II

1) *Read aloud, slowly and prayerfully, the list of ten women from Romans 16. Spend some time thinking of the women who have been influential in your own faith life. These can be personal family and friends, leaders of the present or the past, authors or others who inspired you. Make your own "list of ten" names. It's okay to put some down by role only—as in "sister of Nereus" if you only know them by that, e.g. "the woman who gave up my son for adoption." Come prepared to share these names with those in your group and tell how it felt to create your list.*

2) *Timothy is to Paul the son he never had. Their bonds of affection are evident. Paul speaks highly of the formation Timothy received at the hand of his mother Eunice and his grandmother Lois. His faith is strong both as a Jew initially, and then later as a Christian. While these women are mentioned only referentially through Timothy, most of us would not mind being remembered through the ages for the positive influence we had on our children or grandchildren. Think of your own family tree. Is there a Eunice or a Lois who influenced your life? Is there a Timothy whose life you have influenced?*

3) *Reading all the references to Priscilla and Aquila—and, perhaps, the surrounding text, make a list of what can be known about these two and what you might guess at about them. What questions do you have about them? What impresses you about this married couple in their partnership with Paul? Were you previously aware of their ministry in the early church?*

4) What does the short passage Romans 16:7 tell you about the two people listed? Note that Paul uses the term "apostle" in referring to them. In order to see how Paul felt about the use of the word "apostle," read 1 Cor. 9:1-2 and 1 Cor 15:1-11. Remember that Paul began nearly every letter by identifying himself as the "Apostle to the Gentiles." Given Paul's exalted understanding of what it means to be an apostle, what does this say about these two? How is the second name translated in your translation of the Bible? Come prepared to share the various translations.

5) Write a Midrash as one of these women of the early church.

6) Be prepared to share your response to the CHALLENGE question with your group—in so far as you are comfortable.

CHALLENGE

Have you ever had the experience of working in collaboration with a man in an experience of real partnership? If yes, why did it work, what made it possible? If no, why do you think that experience has not materialized? Do you think it is possible? What part of the problem can women own as their own? Where do you see hope for that possibility?

A CLOSER LOOK AT THE TEXT:
WOMEN IN THE EARLY CHURCH, II

PRISCILLA

The first mention of Rome in Acts comes in the context of Priscilla and Aquila in reference to the expulsion of the Jews by Claudius. As a team they serve as traveling missionaries and are linked to three cities that we know of in scripture, Rome, Corinth and Ephesus. Like Paul, they were tent-makers who worked at their trade. Paul himself wrote describing his lifestyle, "…we are hungry and thirsty, we are poorly clothed and beaten and homeless, and we grow weary from the work of our own hands" (1 Cor. 4:11-12). And in Corinth, where the three worked together, Paul says he was in need to the point of receiving assistance from elsewhere (2 Cor. 11:9). Given this, and the fact that they'd already had to flee a home in Rome, it would be safe to assume that Priscilla and Aquila were not highly placed socio-economically yet commentators frequently refer to them as such because the church met in their house. According to Ivoni Reimer, archeological and inscriptional evidence indicates that the homes serving as house churches could have been very small indeed. So that factor alone would not be sufficient for assigning them to a higher socio-economic class. I mention this because, even as we have been able to identify an androcentric bias in the translation and interpretation of scripture, we need to be aware as educated and wealthy people we can and do bring our own biases to the text as well. We need to be wary that we do not cast others into our own image.

In addition to the trade of tent-making that they shared with Paul, we know that Priscilla and her husband, Aquila, opened their home to Paul in Corinth. Paul describes them in Romans 16 as "fellow workers in the service of Christ" who "even risked their lives for my sake" (vs. 3-4). When Paul decided to move on from Corinth on another mission, Paul took the two of them with him on a sea journey to Ephesus (Acts 18:18).

After but a short stay there he moves on to Caesarea and leaves Priscilla and Aquila in charge of the fledgling church in Ephesus. Later in I Cor 16:1 Paul will refer to them "together with the assembly that meets in their house."

We also know from the Acts 18 that Priscilla and Aquila took on the instruction of Apollos. From the text it is obvious that the three of them, Priscilla, Aquila and Apollos had a good relationship. He came into their home and although he was highly educated, he took no offense at being instructed by this artisan team. This task of teaching Apollos caused Priscilla and Aquila to be remembered and honored in the early church. Historical records have John Chrystostom praise Priscilla for "the whole merit of having instructed Apollos correctly in Christian doctrine." And Tertullian wrote, "By the holy Prisca, the gospel is preached." A church in Rome, "Titulus St. Prisca" is named after her and her name can be found inscribed in the catacombs. The references to Priscilla and Aquila in Paul's own letter (Rom. 16:3-4, 1 Cor. 16:19) reveal both the high esteem he felt for them and their indispensability to his ministry and the ministry of the church in Asia Minor.

There is much that contemporary Christians can learn from Priscilla and Aquila about team ministry, preaching, Eucharistic sharing, and community building. This couple ministry traveled together and created house churches for converts. Priscilla and Aquila modeled partnership in the gospel and a vision of caring community that is as important in our times as it was in their era.

Finding Priscilla in both Paul's writings and Luke's underscores an important characteristic of Acts. Luke's purpose in writing Acts is to focus on Paul. He will always defer to that, especially where women are concerned. References to them are few and sparse. Paul is the one to give more mention to women in his letters.

JUNIA

Paul's reference to Andronicus and Junia as relatives may mean that they were actually members of his family or that they were Jews like him. He describes them as having been in prison with him and as having been members of the church even before he was. The pairing of the names Andronicus and Junia raises the intriguing possibility that, like Priscilla and Aquila, they could have been a married couple. That we cannot know, but it is evident from the text that they ministered as a team and that the women were significant, valued and identified as co-workers, not as wives of.

Most startling, however, is his use of the designation, "apostles." Andronicus and Junia are the only ones besides the twelve and himself to whom Paul gives that name.

What did Paul mean by that? It is not a term Paul uses lightly. Paul claims for himself apostleship status, along with the twelve, in that he also experienced the Risen Christ (*"last of all he was seen by me" 1 Cor. 15:5*) and was commissioned to spread the gospel. He, therefore, expands the word "apostle" beyond the original twelve but reserves it for those who have a specific missionary role borne out by the fruits of their hard labor. We cannot underestimate the weight he gave to that term as we know how vigorously he defended his own title as apostle and how vehemently he opposed those who falsely claimed to be apostles.

Junia was a common female name of the 1st C. and she is cited in patristic sources, e.g. John Chrystostom wrote, "Oh how great is the devotion of this woman that she should be counted worthy of the appellation of apostle!" Similarly, she is also mentioned by Origen, St. Jerome, Hatto of Vercelli, Theophylact and Peter Abelard.

But in the 13th C. the commentator, Aegedius of Rome changed the name, and sex, to Junius—a version lasting down the present time—take a look at the bibles present. (Junia in NRSV, NAB, King James – Junius in New Jerusalem, NIV and Good News).

So the feminine name of Junia was replaced by the masculine form Junius despite the fact that, as a name, there is no other reference to it in literature or records of the ancient world. Apparently the operating logic was that if a woman was referred to as an apostle, she is either not an apostle or not a woman.

PHOEBE

The term Paul uses here for Phoebe is *diakonos*. It is exactly the same term that he uses for Timothy as "our brother and God's *diakonos*" (1 Thes 3:2) and for Tychicus as "our beloved brother and faithful *diakonos*" (Col 4:7). It is not a feminine variation of the word—it is deacon, although even modern translations often render it into deaconess instead of deacon. To speak of a deaconess at this period of church history is an anachronism and is as inaccurate as would be our speaking of plumbers and plumberesses, doctors and doctoresses. (Or, as I recently had a parishioner say, that he and his wife wanted to be an usher and an usherette.)

In addition to being called *diakonos*, she is referred to as prostatis, a word that means leader, chief, president, patron, guardian and protector. But you will frequently find it translated as "being helpful" in various translations of the Bible, a translation that "lightens" the word's impact. Paul recommends Phoebe to the church at Rome with both the terms "deacon" and "benefactor-patron" and he does so without any explanation or apology. This indicates that her role is not a questionable one but, rather, one the community would accept without difficulty.

Paul's commendation of Phoebe at the start indicates that she was the bearer of the letter to the Romans. This is evidence of her work as a traveling missionary, a deacon and a co-worker with Paul. From Paul's letter we cannot ascertain if he merely wanted to assure hospitality for Phoebe or if he had a specific role in mind for her in the church there. Frequently the bearer of the letter also became the one who proclaimed the letter. Given that Paul wrote this before coming to Rome, we are left with the intriguing possibility that while Paul wrote it, it may have been up to Phoebe to explain or teach it— a truly diaconal role.

MEANWHILE, ON SUNDAY MORNING....

Of all the women we have studied, the only one whose name will be read aloud on a Sunday morning is Chloe. On the Third Sunday of Ordinary Time in the "A" Cycle, #68, the second reading comes from II Corinthians and includes vs. 11, "For it has been reported to me by Chloe's people that there are quarrels among you, my brothers and sisters." None of the other women are ever mentioned on a Sunday. There are a couple of times they show up in weekday reading. The listing of names from Romans 16 is read on Saturday of the 31st Week of Ordinary Time, #490 and the reference to Prisca and Aquila from Acts 18:1-3 is read on Thursday of the 6th Week of Easter, #294, and their instruction of Apollos is read on Saturday of the same week, #296.

RESOURCES

WELLHAUSEN'S DOCUMENT THEORY

| PATRIARCHS | | **1900 BCE** |
| | | Myths, Sagas, Songs, Customs |

EXODUS   **1300 c.**
           Oral history, Songs

JUDGES   **1250**
           Legends of the Judges Era

MONARCHY   **1020**   **United Kingdom - Jerusalem**
     J – YAHWIST
           In Judah
           Put together myths, sagas, songs, customs, oral histories and legends of Judges era
           Southern (Judah) point-of-view
           "Yahweh" for God (intimate)
           glorify monarchy & David

           922   **Divided Kingdom**
     E - ELOHIST
           In the Northern Kingdom
           Put together sagas, songs, oral histories
           Northern (Israel) point-of-view
           "Elohim" for God (holy)
           Stress Moses & Covenant

           721   **Assyria conquers N. Kingdom**
     JE
     D – DEUTERONOMIST
           Sources combined
           Additions to *j* and *E*
           J "primitive"
           E linked to land
           Legal traditions
           Stress obedience, faithfulness
           Book of Deuteronomy

EXILE   **587**   **Babylon conquers Judah, Jerusalem destroyed, Leaders deported to Babylon**
     P - PRIESTLY
           Priests gather cultic, legal traditions
           Add law collections to Lev. & Num.

POST-EXILE   **539**   **Cyrus of Persia returns Jews to Israel**
     JEDP   ***P* combines, edits sources**

HAMANTASCHEN

This is a traditional Purim treat that you may want to make when you study Esther. Three-cornered hamantaschen are shaped to resemble the ears of Haman, the villain.

2/3 c. butter
½ c sugar
1 egg
¼ c orange juice (w/o pulp)
1 c white flour
1 c wheat flour
2 tsp baking powder
Various preserves, fruit butters and/or pie fillings

Blend butter and sugar thoroughly. Add the egg and blend thoroughly. Add OJ and blend thoroughly. Add flour, ½ c at a time, alternating white and wheat, blending thoroughly between each. Add the baking powder with the last half cup of flour. Refrigerate dough at least a few hours. Roll thin between two sheets of wax paper lightly dusted with flour. Cut out 3 to 4 inch circles.

Put a dollop of filling in the middle of each circle. Fold up the sides to make a triangle, folding the last corner under the starting point, so that each side has a corner that folds under and a corner that folds over.

Bake at 350 degrees for about 15-20 minutes, until golden brown but before the filling boils over.

Traditional fillings are poppy seed and prune, but apricot is very good—as is apple butter, pineapple preserves and cherry pie filling.

NEVER ON SUNDAY
DAY OF REFLECTION
WOMEN OF HEBREW SCRIPTURES
SAMPLE AGENDA

9:00 GATHERING, WELCOME, REFRESHMENTS
Greet participants, provide refreshments. Once everyone is settle in, provide a simple opening prayer and set the stage for "Laurie King Live."

9:15 INTERVIEW OF THE PROPHET HULDAH
Have two women prepared ahead of time to use the "Laurie King Live" script as interactively as possible.

9:30 SMALL GROUP MIDRASH ACTIVITY
Give directions for everyone to participate in choosing a woman from the First Testament and prepare a midrash to present to the group.

10:15 PRESENTATIONS OF MIDRASHES

11:00 QUIET REFLECTION TIME: WHAT DOES THIS MEAN FOR ME NOW?
Take some time alone to consider the reflection questions and respond.

11:20 SHARING IN PAIRS
Choose a partner (one group of three if you have odd numbers) with whom to share your responses to the reflection questions

11:45 CLOSING PRAYER – A LITANY OF WOMEN
May be followed by lunch together

LAURIE KING INTERVIEWS THE PROPHET HULDAH

LAURIE: Good evening, and welcome to "Laurie King Live." Tonight we are most fortunate to have a prophet as our guest. She is Huldah, who lives in Jerusalem, and has recently been involved in the exciting discovery of a new text at the temple there. Welcome to "Laurie King Live," Huldah.

HULDAH: Thank you, Laurie. It's a pleasure to be here.

LAURIE: Some of our viewers may be surprised to learn that there are women prophets. Are you unusual? Are there others?

HULDAH: Yes, there are many women prophets in our tradition, it is one religious role not limited to men. However, only four women are named as prophets in our Bible. Miriam, she was the first person to be called a prophet,Moses and Aaron's sister. Then there was Deborah, who was a prophet during the time of the Judges, during what you might call our "wild west days." Prophets have always been men and women. I am the third named woman prophet, and the fourth is Noadiah. I know there have been many more who are unnamed.

LAURIE: How did you get to be a prophet?

HULDAH: I was called, just like every other prophet. God calls a prophet; we don't volunteer...

LAURIE: How is it, Huldah, that you became schooled in the scriptures and able to read?

HULDAH: My parents believed that girls should be educated to read and write, as well as boys. So I studied the Scriptures in our home along with my brothers. We were prosperous enough to have a resident scribe in our home, and what you might call a "library," a room where scrolls were kept and where we studied. In our tradition, you never study alone, but with others. My brothers kept me on my toes!

LAURIE: The prophet Isaiah experienced his call while serving in the temple. Were you in the temple when God called you?

HULDAH: No. All prophets receive their call while they are doing their everyday work. Moses was tending his father in law's sheep, for instance. Isaiah was called by God in the temple because he was a priest; during the offering of the sacrifice he was overcome by the incense. In a similar situation, I was called in the kitchen one day while I was cooking chicken soup; overcome, you might say, by the aroma of the soup and the cloud of steam...

LAURIE: We know that you are married, and our listeners might want to know more about your husband. What is it that he does?

HULDAH: He has a prestigious job in the king's court, his title is "keeper of the king's wardrobe." You might say he is in the garment business, a good profession for a Jewish man. He makes sure that all the king's garments are ready to wear--buttons sewn on and hems in place. Of course he has servants to do that, he doesn't do the sewing himself. He goes on buying trips for all the fabrics: purple dyes from Persia, China, linen from Egypt and other fine materials. Has an eye for color that man does. He got this fabric for me from Sheba...

LAURIE: We've heard recently about a new scroll that was discovered, what do you know about that?

HULDAH: You're probably thinking about the recent event in the news, when they were doing temple renovations and came across an ancient scroll of the law. They think it might be the original of the Book of Deuteronomy which is in the Torah.

LAURIE: Huldah, rumors abound about this "lost book." Do you believe it was truly lost all these years or do you think, as some people conjecture, that it was carefully hidden?

HULDAH: Well, I'd have to think about that. Was it truly lost, or did someone hide it? Maybe it was "found" when God intended us to hear it. Sometimes things happen in their own time....

LAURIE: The king sent a delegation to you for your opinion about the scroll. Why do you think the king sought your advice instead of one of the better known male prophets in the city? I understand that the prophet Jeremiah is a contemporary of yours and he is, after all, always in the news.

HULDAH: I really have no idea why the king consulted me. The king, and his advisors, the priests were all stirred up because this scroll said in no uncertain terms that God is angry with us. I've been saying that for awhile: We are not keeping the covenant, people are not keeping kosher kitchens; they aren't even celebrating Passover any more! Why most families in Jerusalem don't even remember the recipe for Matzo Ball Soup! I've been known to complain about all this, so perhaps that's why the king sought me out. Who knows? Maybe the king knew that Jeremiah was depressing, all that doom and gloom, and was hoping for a more upbeat message from me.

LAURIE: That's interesting. Could you give us a sample of your message to the king?

HULDAH: (Unrolls and reads from scroll – 2 Kings 22:15-20)

LAURIE: Were you fearful of predicting such dire consequences to the king?

HULDAH: Not really. Basically there was good news and bad news. The bad news is that the city will be destroyed, but the good news was that the king will die before that happens, so he won't have to experience the destruction. I thought he would take some comfort in that....

LAURIE: What did the king do then, did he listen to your message?

HULDAH: He did. He went into the temple and tore down the shrines to other gods--even took out the booths that the cult prostitutes used. Did you know that they had shrines to other gods in the temple, even had prostitutes, in the temple? Shocking! His actions are known as "Josiah's Reform." This was a real reformation of our religion.

LAURIE: How do you sense what is authentically of God and what is not?

HULDAH: We have a saying in my tradition, that the most important quality of God is hessed, loving kindness. So, I figure that if something is of God it inspires compassion in people, causes them to love one another. But if it does the opposite, causes hate, it is not of God. Our sages tell us that, and so did your Jesus, didn't he? "Love God and love one another" is one way to say it. Or, "What is hateful to you do not do to another."

LAURIE: Why don't we have a "Book of the Prophet Huldah"?

HULDAH: You have to be institutionalized to have a book. You have to have followers to write down your words and keep track of them, and then lobby to get them into the sacred scripture. The system is mostly controlled by the priests and there have never been women priests in our tradition. I've never had connections at the temple at all. Actually, I'm rather pleased that any of my words made it into the Bible!

LAURIE: Thank you so much, Huldah, we are every bit as pleased as you are. Anytime a woman's name, words or story survives, we are truly grateful. Thank you for joining us and for your faithful service to God's word.

Interview created by Libby Goldstein and Kathleen MacInnis Kichline

MIDRASH ACTIVITY

On slips of paper write all the names of the women studied. Have each woman draw a name. OR Make sign-up sheets with all the names of the women from *Never On Sunday*. Participants can choose, singly or in pairs, to sign up for the woman of their choice. Once everyone has their "assignment," use the suggestions below to explore your character and then choose to present her as a story, act as a drama, interview, poem, song, or create a picture.**

1. What is the setting? Where is she?

2. How is the woman dressed? Be specific.

3. What is she doing? What is being done to her?

4. What do you imagine she is feeling and thinking?

5. Is there any dialogue? Between whom? Write it out.

6. What was the significant role this woman played? (In the story, in history, in God's plan)

7. How is she a victim or a hero in this story?

8. What questions would you like to ask her? What does she respond?

9. What do you think is the significance of the woman's name? Is she doesn't have a name, or if you don't know her name, feel free to create one for her as part of your story.

Questions adapted from Women at the Well *by Kathleen Fischer*

**If I were to photograph a flower to represent this woman, what would I photograph, why? What other image represents her? Why?

Supplies to have available might include: various colorful cloths, notepads, colored paper, crayons, paints, ribbons, glue, scissors, leaves, branches, leaves, etc.

NEVER ON SUNDAY

A Look at the Women NOT in the Lectionary

CLOSING PRAYER – A LITANY OF WOMEN

SONG: *(To the tune of "Never On Sunday"—preferably with tambourines)*
You can meet us on a Monday
A Monday, a Monday is very, very good
Or you can meet us on a Tuesday
A Tuesday, a Tuesday, in fact we wish you would
Or you can meet us on a Wednesday,
A Thursday, a Friday, a Saturday's the same
But never, never on a Sunday, a Sunday,
The one day you'll never hear our name.

Come hear our stories; you can do the same
You can tell your stories with no one to blame.
We hear God calling women great and small.
And He still is calling. Can you hear His call?
(back to Refrain)

LEADER: Remember Miriam...
The prophetess Miriam, Aaron's sister, took a tambourine in her hand, while all the women went out after her with tambourines, dancing; and she led them in the refrain: "Sing to the Lord, for he is gloriously triumphant; horse and chariot he has thrown into the sea." (Ex 15:20-21)

ALL: We praise you Miriam, and all women
who lead us with the gift of song.

LEADER: Remember Shiphrah and Puah...

The midwives, however, feared God; they did not do as the king of Egypt had ordered them, but let the boys live. (Exodus 1:17)

ALL: We praise you, Shiphrah and Puah, and all the women
who risk their lives to bring forth new life.

LEADER: Remember Deborah...

"Gone was freedom from beyond the walls, gone indeed from Israel. When I, Deborah, rose, when I rose, a mother in Israel...Awake, awake Deborah! Awake, awake, stir up a song." (Judges 5:7,12)

ALL: We praise you Deborah, and all women
who have the wisdom to lead others with justice

LEADER: Remember Ruth and Naomi...

"Do not ask me to abandon or forsake you! For wherever you go I will go, wherever you lodge I will lodge, your people shall be my people, and your God my God. Wherever you die I will die and there be buried. May the Lord do so and so to me, and more besides, if aught but death separates me from you!" (Ruth 1:16-17)

ALL: We praise you Ruth and Naomi, and all women
who face the future with hope

LEADER: Remember Huldah...

So Hildiah the priest, Ahikam, Achbor, Shaphn, and Asaiah betook themselves to the Second Quarter in Jerusalem, where the prophetess Huldah resided. She was the wife of Shallum, son of Tikvah, son of Harhas, keeper of the wardrobe. When they had spoken to her, she said to them, "Thus says the Lord, the God of Israel...." (2 Kings 22:14-15)

ALL: We praise you Huldah, and all women
who have vision to see the future for our people.

LEADER: Remember Esther...

Then Esther said in reply to Mordecai, "Go, gather all the Jews to be found in Susa, and hold a fast on my behalf, and neither eat nor drink for three days, night or day. I and my maids will also fast as you do. After that I will go to the king, though it is against the law; and if I perish, I perish." (Esther 4:15-16)

ALL: We praise you Esther, and all women
who use their status to intervene for those who are in peril.

LEADER: Remember Judith...

"O God, my God, hear me also, a widow. It is you who were the author of those events and of what preceded and followed them. The present, also, and the future you have planned. Whatever you devise comes into being; the things you decide on come forward and say, 'Here we are!' All your ways are in readiness, and your judgment is made with foreknowledge." (Judith 9:5-6)

ALL: We praise you Judith, and all women
              who confront evil with courage and grace.

ALL: O Spirit of the Living God,
              Your wisdom is reflected in the stories of our sisters
              and your power is made manifest in the outlines of their lives.
              You were there when they stood for justice,
              and you rode with them into battle against all the evil forces
              that surrounded them and still surround us.
              Be with us now as we too face the hour of our decision.
              Make us strong, secure, confident that you will achieve what we must do.
              We praise your name and we thank you in the name of all women.
              Amen.

συνέρχεσθαι

NEVER ON SUNDAY
DAY OF REFLECTION
WOMEN OF CHRISTIAN SCRIPTURES
SAMPLE AGENDA

9:00 GATHERING, WELCOME, REFRESHMENTS
Greet participants, provide refreshments.

9:15 OPENING PRAYER

9:30 SMALL GROUP MIDRASH ACTIVITY
See instructions for this same exercise in earlier Reflection Day:
Women of the Hebrew Scriptures

10:15 PRESENTATIONS OF MIDRASHES

11:00 HOW HAS WHAT I'VE LEARNED AND EXPERIENCE IN THIS STUDY
IMPACTED MY FAITH LIFE TODAY?
Quiet time to reflect, pray upon and journal your response to this question.

11:20 SHARING IN PAIRS
Choose a partner (one group of three if the number is odd) with whom
you can share your responses to the reflection question.

11:45 CLOSING PRAYER

NOTES FOR FACILITATORS: *This Day of Reflection mirrors the earlier one for the* Women of the Hebrew
Scriptures. *You may well, then, be able on your last day to have the participants draw the names for their midrashes
then. This could help them anticipate the retreat event.*

*For the environment create a focal point with cloths, candle, and bible. Have a collection of smooth stones in
a basket as well as one larger stone on which is inscribed the Icthys Fish or is simply lettered JESUS.*

DAY OF REFLECTION OPENING PRAYER

LEADER: Lord, we thank you for bringing us to this time and place and ask you to bless our time together. Open our minds to receive your inspiration, our hearts to respond with love, our lips to speak your truth and our eyes to recognize you in the many ways you reveal yourself in our midst.

LECTOR: John 10:1-5

LEADER: We have spent this year learning about women whose stories we have never heard on a Sunday. These past weeks we have focused on women who knew Jesus, who served, loved and followed him, as do we. We remember that electric moment when Jesus spoke aloud the name, "Mary!" and Mary of Magdala recognized her risen Lord and Savior. We, too, are called by Jesus and called by name. As I call each of you by name, I ask you to come forward, choose a stone and place it alongside the Jesus Rock.

Slowly read each name in turn and allow the women time to come forward, choose a stone and place in by the rock. (Soft music may be playing)

LECTOR: Matthew 18:19-20

LEADER: We gather, Jesus, in your name and we pray together in your name. We come, each of us, with the awareness of others in our hearts. Some of these are people we are praying for, some of these are people we are grateful for, some of these are people whom God calls to mind in the moment. I invite all of you to come forward as the Spirit moves you, choose a stone for that person and speak aloud his or her name as you add that stone to the others. You may choose more than one stone/person.

Allow time for each person to respond.

When everyone has been "named," pray:

LEADER: We thank you for having called each of us by name, for loving each of us so extravagantly. We place ourselves, now in your presence and all those whom we love into your care. AMEN.

You may want to end with a song, e.g. The Summons, In This Place, We Are Called, *etc.*

DAY OF REFLECTION CLOSING PRAYER

LEADER: Let us add to our circle of witnesses these women of whom we hear *Never On Sunday* but who have are real and present to us here today.

LEADER: Remember **Mary of Nazareth**...*place a stone with the Jesus rock*

LECTOR: And Mary said, "My soul magnifies the Lord, and my spirit rejoices in God my Savior, for he has looked with favor on the lowliness of his servant. Surely, from now on all generations will call me blesses; for the Mighty One has done great things for me and holy is his name." (Luke 1:46-49).

ALL: We praise you holy woman of God; by your faithful witness the Church is made whole.

LEADER: Remember the woman bent over...*place a stone with the Jesus rock*

LECTOR: There was a woman there who for eighteen years had been possessed by a spirit which drained her strength. She was badly stooped and quite incapable of standing erect. When Jesus saw her, he called her to him and said, "Woman, you are free of your infirmity." He laid his hand on her, and immediately she stood up straight and beganpraising God. (Lk. 13: 11-13).

ALL: We praise you holy woman of God; by your faithful witness the Church is made whole.

LEADER: Remember the women who followed Jesus: ...*place a stone with the Jesus rock as each name is read*

Mary, wife of Clopas the sister of Mary
Mary, the mother of James and Joses
Salome, wife of Zebedee and mother of James and John
Joanna, wife of Chuza
Susanna
Mary of Magdala
Mary, mother of Jesus,
"many others who provided for them out of their means."

LECTOR: Many women were also there, looking on from a distance; they had followed Jesus from Galilee and had provided for him. (Mt. 27:55)

ALL: We praise you holy women of God; by your faithful witness the Church is made whole.

LEADER: Mary Magdalene...*place a stone with the Jesus rock*

LECTOR: Jesus said to her, "Mary!" She turned to him and said "Rabbouni!" Jesus then said: "Do not cling to me, for I have not yet ascended to the Father. Rather, go to my brothers and tell them, "I am ascending to my Father and your Father, to my God and your God!" Mary Magdalene went to the disciples. "I have seen the Lord," she announced.

ALL: We praise you holy woman of God; by your faithful witness the Church is made whole.

LEADER: Remember the women in the early church: ...*place a stone with the Jesus rock as each name is read*

Tabitha or Dorcas
Mary, the mother of John Mark
Rhoda Lydia Phoebe Priscilla Mary Junia
Tyrphanea Tryphosa Persis
Mother of Rufus
Julia
Sister of Nereus
Apphia
Chloe
Claudia Damaris Lois Eunice Eudoia Syntyche
Give my greetings to Prisca and Aquila; they were my fellow workers in the service of Christ Jesus and even risked their lives for the sake of mine. Not only I but all the churches of the Gentiles are grateful to them. (Rom. 16:3-4).

ALL: We praise you holy women of God; by your faithful witness the Church is made whole.

LECTOR: 1 Peter 4-5

LEADER: Let us pray together the second Prayer of the Women in the Early Church:

PRAYER OF
THE WOMEN IN THE EARLY CHURCH, II

We thank you, Lord, for the example of these holy women.

We thank you that you entrusted to them the building up of your church.

May we be as faithful in teaching, serving, encouraging and in spreading the word of your Kingdom.

It is too easy, Lord, to think it was once simpler or better.

We are the women you choose to use today.

We are born in this time and this place that we might make it holy, that we might bring about your Kingdom in the here and now.

Nor would you ask us anything without gifting us for the task. Stir within us the confidence to act in your name.

Inspire within us a great desire to know you, to follow you and to share your love with others.

May the Church you love be made better and more faithful to your vision by receiving the gifts we offer.

Amen.

- KMcK

SAMPLE MIDRASH

JOCHEBED

I, Jochebed, a God-fearing woman of the tribe of Levi, have a story to tell you—such a story! I remember as if it happened yesterday. I was blessed with three children—Miriam, Aaron and an infant son. But it was hard times then to have children, living, as we were, as slaves in Egypt. The Pharaoh feared our numbers and thought we might rebel. So he ordered the midwives to kill all male babies born to Hebrew women. But two midwives defied the order and our babies were spared. So it was with my first son, Aaron.

But then Pharaoh issued the general command that all Hebrew baby boys be thrown into the river to drown. It was then my second son was born and we feared for his life. I kept him hidden for three months but was always fearful that we would be discovered and harm would come to us all. I was so torn and so fearful and I pleaded with my husband to do something. He, too, was full of fear and, really, what could he do? What can I do, I asked myself, I cannot let my son die. I must think clearly. I must keep calm, I must come up with something practical that will keep my son alive and everyone around us safe. My husband will not do anything, but I must. I am his mother. I am afraid but I will pray to think clearly and I will put my faith in my God to guide me.

What shall I do? Can I send him away? But where? To whom? How? The river... Yes, the river. But not to drown as the Pharaoh commands. Oh, he is so cruel. Hmm, Pharaoh's daughter. She has a reputation of being compassionate and kind and she seems to like children. But will she help me? Think...pray...think. God is in control and I am under God's control. I must be calm. I cannot approach her; it is not seemly. But if she happens to find a baby....I know she will help. How can this happen? I will bring him to her in the castle. No. I will put him in the river—in a basket, a papyrus basket and I will line it with pitch and tar so that it will float. Then I will put it among the reeds near where she bathes and I will pray she finds it when she goes to the river. Now, I have a plan and, with God's help, I pray it will work. I need to tell my husband, the first hurdle I must face. Then Miriam, my daughter, Miriam, I will send her to watch the basket and see what happens.

And, so, after much arguing and pleading on my part, my husband agreed to my plan and with many tears from all of us, we bundled up our infant son and gave him to Miriam to take to the river. Some time later, Miriam returned home. Pharaoh's daughter had found my baby and she asked Miriam to find an available wetnurse among the Hebrew women. And that is me!! I AM TO NURSE MY OWN SON! She will even pay me. And I will keep him for four years and will be able to teach him about his God and his heritage. And he will know his family. Praise God, Lord of the universe.

Is God good? I will love my son and I will teach him well. It will be hard knowing that he will go to Pharaoh's daughter in time. But I will have my son for a little while. He will not be killed. I can do it. God will help me.

And so it was that for four years, this child lived with his family. And he was loved and I taught him all that I thought was important for him to know. Then he was taken to Pharaoh's daughter and he became her son. She named him Moses and he was given all the privileges and education of a wealthy Egyptian. And he did not forget us, did not forget his heritage. He became a man who served his God and his people. He was always my son. Thank you for listening to my story of how God the prayers of this mother.

NAOMI AND RUTH

After Ruth's week of confinement from the baby's birth, it was the evening before his bris when he would receive his name and be circumcised. The women had gathered to celebrate with Ruth. When they entered the tent they saw Mara with Ruth sitting at her feet, holding her infant son. They were a little surprised as the mother-in-law is not usually included in this customary celebration. Ruth rose to greet her guests and put the babe in one of the women's arms. She busied herself pouring wine from a skin for everyone.

Mara called out to her, "Do not dilute the wine with too much water. This is going to be a real party!" This was met with laughter and merriment. The ladies enjoyed the wine and some special foods that Mara had been preparing since the baby's birth. It was only a portion of what would be served at the bris on the morrow. The ladies passed the baby around, each enjoying the smell of a newborn, along with the food, wine, and fellowship.

Everyone was laughing, feeling good and having a wonderful time when Mara stood and called for their attention. She told them that now she was to be called Naomi again. Mara was someone of the past. Her life was once again pleasant, more than pleasant! She said that God had blessed her with a wonderful daughter-in-law and a beautiful baby boy and happiness in her old age. She broke down at the end of her speech, tearfully thanking Ruth will all of her tears.

Ruth rose from her rug and took the baby from a friend. She hugged Naomi and whispered something to her. There wasn't a dry eye in the tent. She then walked to the middle of the group and said that they were going to stray from tradition. The baby's name was normally kept a secret for the first eight days of his life, but she asked all of the women to help her name her darling son.

After a brief silence, they started tossing out names. They discussed possibilities from the list of ancients. They discussed names that they had heard from visitors from other lands that had spent a night or two in their camp over the years. They mentioned names from all the Great: Abraham, Isaac, Jacob, Judah, Perez. They discussed variations of Lot, Joseph, Moses, Noah, or even variations of their wives' names: Sarah, Rebecca, Leah, Rachel, Tamar, or even Ruth and Naomi. They asked Ruth of names from Moab and about Naomi's sons' names. They talked and laughed and shared the stories that had been handed down to them. The moon traveled across the sky and someone remarked that the East was beginning to grow light.

Ruth whispered to her best friends to join her, each holding a bit of the baby's blanket, and they carefully laid the baby in Naomi's arms. Ruth told the group that the baby was Naomi's to name.

Since it was the day of the bris, Naomi could tell the group the name she chose. But first, she swore them to secrecy until after the circumcision was completed. She raised the baby up over her head and told them that the name she was choosing was because she'd had a vision. This child would become a holy man, perhaps a leader or judge or priest. He name meant "servant, worshipper." His name was Obed. Obe became the next in the lineage of the Greats, for 42 generations to the Messiah!

That is how God blessed both Ruth and Naomi for their faithfulness and loyalty to the covenant of love.

HULDAH

When I was a small girl, my father called me Hulda, "little ferret." He meant it as a compliment, since, in his eyes, the best thing a person could do was to "ferret out," or search for the underlying meaning of words, of things, of people. Because I kept pestering him, he taught me how to read, although it was an unusual thing that a girl child be taught to read in my day. My father couldn't refuse me when I scurried to get my household chores done in order to study the Holy Books with him. I learned many things from my earthly father. I learned faithfulness to Yahweh and I learned to tell the truth, not matter who was watching. As I saw the way my father dealt with others, I learned the meaning of kindness. I learned that people need to be treated fairly.

As a married woman, growing older, I learned the blessing of children and to pass on the truths I'd been given by my heavenly father. I watched, with horror, those who struck down innocent babies, fearing that their God would not allow our crops to yield abundantly unless we appeased him with the sacrifice of innocents. How many times I watched these practices and wondered how their idea of God could be so different from my own. I prayed and listened until my heart-strings echoed with God's melody of life. Only when the same notes played within me could I be at peace. People called me wise; they called me "prophetess," as I called them to find God's melody within their own hearts.

And now, I am an old woman who is called to decide if this book, found in the Jerusalem temple, contains the words of God, written for his people. Could this be a forgery, written by those who were so fearful that they lived only to appease an angry, vengeful God? It's a great responsibility and I've asked for God to help me, to touch the strings of my heart with his voice so that his harmonies will echo within me. As I read the legends, the stories of the covenant made by God and his people, I remembered the wisdom passed on to me by my earthly father. Surely, these were the words of our God, the one who wants to be in relationship with us, the one who tells us we are made in God's own image. If I could not abide the killing of innocent children, sacrificed to Molech, and I am made in the image of God, how could Yahweh, this God of mine, do less? Surely, these are the words of God's Covenant of hope for us all.